ADVANCES IN COACH EDUCATION AND DEVELOPMENT

This book highlights the latest advances in coach education and development through collaborative research co-ordinated by The English Football Association (The FA), the only national governing body of sport to run a coaching research programme. *Advances in Coach Education and Development* presents the first set of studies generated by this programme that display how research has informed policy and practice within The FA.

Divided into three parts, each investigates an aspect of this programme such as The FA's coaching education and development provision, its commitment to developing the developer and how its coaches put their knowledge into practice. Each chapter includes sections that examine current issues, suggest considerations for other governing bodies and pose key questions, including:

- What can other governing bodies learn from The FA's programme?
- What is the best way to capture and compare different coaching systems?
- How can other organisations optimise success within their coach education and development programmes?
- How can future research continue to unpack and understand the complex role of coach educators?

Bringing together a unique set of studies covering every level of football, from elite to grassroots, this book is essential reading for any serious sports coaching student, researcher or coach educator.

Wayne Allison is Coaching Research Manager within the Technical Directorate at The English Football Association, UK.

Andrew Abraham is a Principal Lecturer and Academic Group Leader in Sports Coaching at Leeds Beckett University, UK.

Andy Cale is a Principal Lecturer in Sports Coaching at the University of Worcester, UK.

ADVANCES IN COACH EDUCATION AND DEVELOPMENT

From research to practice

Edited by Wayne Allison,
Andrew Abraham and Andy Cale

 **Routledge**
Taylor & Francis Group

LONDON AND NEW YORK

First published 2016
by Routledge
2 Park Square, Milton Park, Abingdon, Oxon OX14 4RN

and by Routledge
711 Third Avenue, New York, NY 10017

Routledge is an imprint of the Taylor & Francis Group, an informa business

British Library Cataloguing-in-Publication Data
A catalogue record for this book is available from the British Library

Library of Congress Cataloging in Publication Data
Names: Allison, Wayne, editor. | Football Association (England)
Title: Advances in coach education and development : from research to practice / edited by Wayne Allison, Andrew Abraham, Andy Cale.
Description: New York : Routledge, 2016. | Includes bibliographical references and index.
Identifiers: LCCN 2015039777 | ISBN 9781138100787 (Hardback) | ISBN 9781138100794 (Paperback) | ISBN 9781315657486 (Ebook)
Subjects: LCSH: Soccer coaches--Training of--Great Britain. | Soccer--Coaching--Great Britain. | Coaching (Athletics)--Great Britain. | Coaching (Athletics)--Study and teaching.
Classification: LCC GV943.8 .A38 2016 | DDC 796.33407/7--dc23
LC record available at http://lccn.loc.gov/2015039777

ISBN: 978-1-138-100787 (hbk)
ISBN: 978-1-138-100794 (pbk)
ISBN: 978-1-315-657486 (ebk)

Typeset in Bembo
by Saxon Graphics Ltd, Derby
Printed in Great Britain by Ashford Colour Press Ltd

MIX
Paper from
responsible sources
FSC
www.fsc.org
FSC® C011748

In memory of Pat Duffy
A great friend, colleague and innovator

CONTENTS

PART IV
Summary

ILLUSTRATIONS

Figures

Tables

PREFACE

The aims and structure of this book

The purpose of the book and the reasons for writing it

The aim of this book is to highlight and communicate the advances made in coach education and development through collaborative research co-ordinated by The English Football Association (The FA) examining the complex nature of coaching. The novel research focuses on the ambiguous, political and very personal nature of coaching and coach education practice (Jones, 2006). In this regard, and from a sport national governing body (NGB) perspective, we hope to problematise everyday processes in coaching and coach education to display how research has uniquely informed policy and practice within The FA.

The concepts in this book are intended to enhance understanding and refinement of the role of the coach and their education through developing more discerning strategies to deal with the complexity and constraints inherent in these processes. It is hoped that improved conceptual insight and clarity will lead to increased knowledge and understanding of effective coaching, building on earlier work by Jones *et al.* (2004) and Cassidy *et al.* (2004).

The book is intended to make coaches and coach educators reflect on theoretical concepts, thus providing options to think in different ways about their practice and its consequences. Ultimately, the text seeks to assist in the improvement of understanding and discretion in coaches and coach educators, to provoke thought, questions and discussion as to why they coach the way they do. In going beyond the known, it is concerned with developing more realistic analysis and better understanding of what coaches actually do, while suggesting ways of helping their performance and education (Jones, 2006).

The scope and contents of the book

The book brings together a number of internationally reputable sports-related scholars to investigate coaching, coach education and development. It is important to note that the contributions contain new knowledge and not simply re-written material from previous work. The book is divided into three principal parts. Following an introductory chapter (Chapter 1), the first part (Chapters 2–4) contains research about contextual issues in coach education and development. The second part (Chapters 5–7) primarily focuses on The FA's commitment to supporting the coach developer or educator. The third part (Chapters 8–13) contains detailed investigations into the impact on practice. Finally, Chapter 14 provides a summary and highlights important considerations with implications for future directions. It frames the theories presented in the book as threshold concepts (Toole & Seashore Louis, 2002), which can act as signposts to new ways of seeing and understanding.

The intended level of readership

The book is primarily aimed at coaches and coach educators working in football and other sports, as well as academic specialists and undergraduate and postgraduate students of coaching. The book has been specifically designed so that each chapter can be used independently as a reference guide. The different, but linked, chapters provide a methodological/conceptual approach that can be easily adopted, with the intention to either develop or substantiate good practice or build on and improve existing coach education and development programmes.

It is anticipated that the reader will appreciate that coaching is an inherently non-routine, problematic and complex endeavour in which a large amount of untapped, tacit knowledge already exists in players and coaches. In addition, coaching is an activity primarily based on social interaction and power, where the challenges that coaches encounter are partly localised and must be addressed 'on the ground' (Toole & Seashore Louis, 2002).

References

Cassidy, T., Jones, R. & Potrac, P. (2004). *Understanding sports coaching: the social, cultural and pedagogical foundations of coaching practice.* Abingdon: Routledge.

Jones, R. (2006). *The sports coach as educator: reconceptualising sports coaching.* London: Routledge.

Jones, R., Armour, K. & Potrac, P. (2004). *Sports coaching cultures: from practice to theory.* London: Routledge.

Toole, J.C. & Seashore Louis, K. (2002). The role of professional learning communities in international education. In K. Leithwood and P. Hallinger (eds), *Second international handbook of educational leadership and administration.* London: Kluwer Publishers.

ACKNOWLEDGEMENTS

We would like to thank: The English Football Association for allowing us to share what we consider as best practice research in coach education and development; the authors, who have demonstrated ultimate professionalism in producing chapters of the highest quality; and Simon Whitmore from Routledge for believing in this project and for providing invaluable support in the completion of this book.

CONTRIBUTORS

Andrew Abraham, PhD, is a Principal Lecturer in Sport Coaching at Leeds Beckett University. He has 17 years' experience in researching coaching and coach education. He has been involved in writing numerous degrees and postgraduate qualifications in the area of sport coaching and coach education. Most recently he has been engaged in researching and creating a bespoke postgraduate qualification in coach education for The English Football Association. Andrew has written numerous book chapters, papers and professional reports. He is a reviewer for the *Journal of Sport Sciences* and has reviewed papers for several other coaching journals.

Wayne Allison, PhD, is the Coaching Research Manager for The English Football Association. He is responsible for providing the underpinning knowledge of research to inform policy that can then be practically applied to support and enhance coach education and development. A former professional footballer, who made over 870 appearances for clubs including Bristol City, Swindon Town, Huddersfield Town, Sheffield United and Chesterfield, Wayne has a PhD in Sport Exercise Science and Coaching and holds the full range of UEFA Coaching qualifications, including the UEFA Pro Licence. He has also been Assistant Manager at Chester City and been on the coaching staff at Bury, Tranmere Rovers and Bradford City.

Paul Appleton, PhD, is a Research Fellow at the University of Birmingham, working on projects related to Empowering Coaching™. At Birmingham, Paul also leads the Motivation in Sport and Exercise undergraduate module. He has published his work in several leading journals in the field. Paul also serves as a regular reviewer for various international peer-reviewed journals and has presented his research at national and international conferences.

Kathleen Armour is Professor of Education & Sport and Head of the School of Sport, Exercise and Rehabilitation Sciences at the University of Birmingham. Her research focuses on professional learning and career-long professional development for teachers and coaches. Kathy has a particular interest in finding new mechanisms to bridge the gaps between research and practice in order to change both.

Jake Bailey is a Principal Lecturer in Sports Coaching in the Cardiff School of Sport, Cardiff Metropolitan University, whose research interests lie in the sociology of sports coaching. He is involved in coach development, and is particularly interested in the design, implementation and evaluation of coach education projects. Jake is an active gymnastics coach and is a mentor for British Gymnastics on their High Performance Coach Development Programme.

Steven Bradbury, PhD, is a Lecturer in Young People and Sport at the School of Sport, Exercise and Health Sciences, Loughborough University. He has a strong track record in undertaking and publishing research around issues of 'race', ethnicity and sport, with particular regard to professional and amateur football in the UK and Europe. To this end, his research has focused mainly on examining the levels of representation and experiences of BME participants from youth and adult populations across the playing, coaching and governance tiers of the game.

Andy Cale, PhD, is a Principal Lecturer at the University of Worcester, involved in Inclusive Coaching, Coach Education and Development. Andy has worked in football and education for well over 25 years and brings a unique combination that blends high-level practical experience as a Coach (UEFA Pro Licence holder), Manager and Sport Psychologist with a strong academic foundation. Having initially qualified from Loughborough University, Andy has enjoyed a career with many different organisations, including: Sheffield United as a Sports Psychologist, The Football Association as Head of Player Development and Research, The New Saints (TNS) as a Manager in the Champions League.

Alexander De Lyon is a Doctoral Researcher in the School of Sport, Exercise and Rehabilitation Sciences at the University of Birmingham. The main focus of his research is on the professional training, development and work practices of the fitness industry workforce in the UK. In the context of sport, Alex has contributed to professional development research projects for major national governing bodies, and he has presented his research both nationally and internationally.

Joan Duda is a Professor of Sport and Exercise Psychology at the University of Birmingham. Joan is internationally known for her expertise on motivational processes and determinants of optimal functioning in sport, exercise and dance, and is one of the most cited researchers in her field (with more than 250 publications to her name). She also has extensive experience as a Sport Psychology Consultant working with world-class athletes and Olympic teams. Joan has created the theory-

and evidence-based Empowering Coaching™ family of training programmes which are being delivered to coaches, parents and teachers in the UK and abroad.

Hayley Fitzgerald, PhD, is a Reader in Disability and Youth Sport at Leeds Beckett University and teaches on a range of undergraduate and postgraduate modules focusing on social and cultural aspects of leisure, sport and physical education. Hayley's research interests are primarily in the area of disability, physical education and youth sport. Hayley is committed to including all young disabled people within research and evaluation work. She has extensive experience of developing accessible and participatory research strategies. She edited the Routledge text *Disability and Youth Sport* and is on the editorial board of *Adapted Physical Activity Quarterly*.

Paul R. Ford, PhD, is a Senior Lecturer at the University of Brighton and Honorary Researcher at Liverpool John Moores University. He has been funded to research and published regularly in the areas of expert performance, skill acquisition, learning, coaching and football. He has worked as a consultant in his specialist areas in professional football with clubs and governing bodies, as well as in other elite sports. He holds High Performance Sport Accreditation from the British Association of Sport and Exercise Sciences and a Teaching Fellowship from the Higher Education Funding Council for England.

Mark Griffiths, PhD, is a Lecturer in the School of Sport, Exercise and Rehabilitation Sciences at the University of Birmingham. His research is located in the area of Sport Pedagogy and focuses on understanding and improving theory and practice in sport, physical activity and physical education. Mark has a specific interest in the way that coaches and teachers engage with different learning activities, and the factors that promote or obstruct their learning engagement.

Ryan Groom, PhD, is Programme Leader for the MA/MSc Exercise and Sport postgraduate degree at Manchester Metropolitan University, Cheshire, leading and teaching modules on research methods and coach education. He has previously worked for a number of Premier League and England international football teams in the area of performance analysis. His main research interest is in exploring qualitative research methodologies and theory, particularly within education and sports coaching. His work is based predominantly on working within naturalistic and ethnographic frameworks exploring the complexities of practice. He has lead and collaborated a number of funded research projects with Sport England, the English Institute of Sport, British Canoeing and The English Football Association. He has also co-edited two Routledge texts, *Research Methods in Sports Coaching* and *Learning in Sports Coaching*.

Robyn L. Jones is a Professor of Sport and Social Theory at the Cardiff School of Sport, Cardiff Metropolitan University, a Visiting Professor (II) at the Norwegian School of Sport Sciences, Oslo (Research) and a Visiting Associate Principal Lecturer at Hartpury College, UK. His research area comprises a critical sociology of coaching in respect of examining the complexity of the interactive coaching context and how practitioners manage the power-ridden dilemmas that arise. He has (co-)published in excess of 60 peer-reviewed articles and several books on sports coaching and pedagogy. In addition to serving on the editorial board of *Sport, Education and Society*, Robyn is also the General Editor of the Taylor & Francis journal *Sports Coaching Review*. During the past 15 years he has served in numerous consultancy (coach education) positions including those for The Football Association, the Welsh Rugby Union and High Performance Sport New Zealand.

Ellie May is a final-year PhD student at Leeds Beckett University. Ellie's PhD research gained International Paralympic Committee approval and explores volunteerism at the London 2012 Paralympic Games. This research offers insights into the profiles of volunteers while also exploring volunteers' understandings and perceptions of disability, disability sport and 'disabled' athletes. Theoretically, this research draws on critical disability studies and notions of social capital. Ellie also has experience of lecturing on a variety of sports studies and events management courses and offering research assistance to a broad range of volunteering, sport and health-related research projects.

Jenny Moon is an Associate Professor at Bournemouth University in the Centre for Excellence in Media Practice. Jenny has worked in education, health and professional development in higher education. In recent years, her focus has been on pedagogy, with an interest in how humans learn (reflective learning, critical thinking, academic assertiveness, the role of story in education). Jenny also runs workshops at universities over the UK, Ireland and abroad. She covers a range of topics. These include reflective learning, the use of learning journals to support learning and professional development, critical thinking, issues in cheating and plagiarism, academic assertiveness and the role of story in higher education and oral storytelling.

Julian North is a Senior Research Fellow in the Carnegie School of Sport at Leeds Beckett University. Most of his recent research work has focused on football. He has led projects investigating player development and coaching in the performance pathway for The English FA and UEFA. He has also led a Europe-wide review of UEFA's Coaching Convention. Julian has 20 years' research experience working for a range of private, public and higher education organisations, including the Australian Institute of Sport, UK Sport and Sports Coach UK. He is a qualified football coach working with a large community club in the Leeds area.

Paul Potrac is a Professor of Sports Coaching within the Department of Sport and Physical Activity at Edge Hill University and an Honorary Professor at the University of Hull. Paul's research focuses on the political and emotional features of everyday life in coaching and coach education settings. He has (co-)published several books, including *Sports Coaching Cultures*, *The Routledge Handbook of Sports Coaching*, *Research Methods in Sports Coaching* and *A Sociology of Sports Coaching*. Paul is also an Associate Editor of the Taylor and Francis journal *Sports Coaching Review*.

Eleanor Quested, PhD, is a Senior Research Fellow at Curtin University, Australia. Previously, Eleanor was at the University of Birmingham, where she was Research Fellow and Manager of the PAPA (Promoting Adolescent Physical Activity; www. projectpapa.org) project. PAPA further developed and tested the Empowering Coaching™ programme in five European countries. Eleanor's research focuses on the social–environmental and motivational processes associated with adaptive, health-conducive physical activity participation across the lifespan. Eleanor has published in leading sport psychology journals and presented at national and international conferences. She has lectured in sport/dance psychology and delivered motivation-related workshops to athletes, dancers and teachers.

Annette Stride, PhD, is a Senior Lecturer at Leeds Beckett University, teaching across the Sport Business Management and Physical Education undergraduate and postgraduate degree programmes. Her research has a social justice agenda, working with groups often marginalised or disadvantaged within physical education and activity contexts. More specifically, she is interested in how the connections between gender and other identity markers including ethnicity, disability and sexuality influence young people's involvement in and engagement with PE and physical activity. Within her research, Annette draws on a range of innovative, creative and participatory research methods to engage with her participants.

William Taylor, PhD, works in the Department of Exercise and Sport Science at Manchester Metropolitan University, Cheshire. His research interests are eclectic and include: coaching in the risk society; the application of post-structuralist theory in examining coaching relations; and the development of professionalism and professional practice. He has undertaken a number of funded research projects for bodies such as England Hockey, British Canoeing, English Institute of Sport, Economic and Social Research Council, Sport England, Sports Coach UK and The English Football Association. An ex-international canoe sport competitor, he continues to coach mainly on the development and delivery of coach education programmes. He recently co-edited a Routledge text, *Moral Panic in Physical Education and Coaching* (2015).

Jordan Whelan is currently a Doctor of Philosophy candidate in the School of Sport and Exercise Sciences at Liverpool John Moores University, UK. His research is in the areas of expert performance, skill acquisition, performance analysis and coaching. His doctoral thesis examines decision-making in football and its acquisition through coaching. He graduated BSc (Hons) Science and Football from Liverpool John Moores University in 2013. He currently works as a performance analyst at Liverpool FC and as a tutor for the education courses of Prozone.

1

THE FA'S COACH EDUCATION AND DEVELOPMENT PROGRAMME

Research informing practice

Wayne Allison

Introduction

The aim of this chapter is to illustrate how The FA is attempting to establish a research culture of inclusivity and collaboration with research experts and higher education (HE). The chapter outlines the processes taken towards this goal, as well as detailing how The FA's coach education and development programme has evolved and advanced across time. Several process models are presented that exemplify how coaching research is conducted at The FA, which could assist other national governing bodies (NGBs) in the formation and development of their own research procedures. The chapters contained in this book demonstrate the outcomes of this research process.

The FA coach education: from past to present

Traditionally, The FA's coach education and development programme was centred on football coaching and involved the attainment of qualifications recognised and awarded solely by The FA. The FA Preliminary Award and Full Badge awards were delivered from 1946 until 1996, after which the Junior Team Manager, Coaching Certificate and Coaching License were awarded for Levels 1, 2 and 3, respectively. More recently, The FA recognised that in order to further support excellent coaches, the coach education pathway should be updated. Following a review, the pathway was refreshed in 2003–4 with The FA Level 1 and Level 2 courses being placed on the former National Qualifications Framework and accreditation achieved for the Union of European Football Associations (UEFA) 'B', UEFA 'A' and UEFA Pro Licence courses. UK Coaching Certificate (UKCC) accreditation (a Sports Coach UK initiative that supports the development, endorsement and continuous improvement of the governing body of sport coach education programmes) was also achieved for Level 1 and Level 2, recognising the status of football awards and The FA's commitment to coach education and development and the UKCC principles.

Refinements to the coach education and development programme continued, culminating in the publication of The Future Game document in 2010, The FA Technical Guide for Young Player Development, which outlined a philosophy and vision for the future of youth development in English football. Key parts of the philosophy were the principles of creativity and innovation for both coaches and players and playing philosophy based on quality passing, possession and 'building play' through three-thirds of the pitch.

There were numerous reasons that prompted publication of The Future Game document. At the highest level of the male game, there was a belief that English players were inferior to their global counterparts with regards to technical competence and decision-making capability. Furthermore, with the development of the Premier League and the significant influence of foreign coaches and players, the culture of English professional football had changed significantly to that in the early 1990s. European and international football, the arena in which young English players were competing, had also advanced (The Future Game, 2010).

Therefore, in order to communicate the messages from The Future Game and to meet the developmental needs of the coaches operating in youth development, The FA introduced a series of new awards, The FA Youth Award Modules 1, 2 and 3 and the Advanced Youth Award (equivalent to the UEFA 'A' Licence award). The FA Youth Award Modules 1, 2 and 3 together with the UEFA 'B' Licence are now the minimum mandatory qualification requirements for coaches working in the Professional Youth Academies as part of the Elite Player Performance Plan (EPPP) introduced by the Premier League in 2010.

The EPPP is a long-term plan that promotes the development of a world-leading youth academy system. It details the processes and criteria necessary to ensure that professional football in England is empowered to create a world-leading academy system that provides more and better home-grown players and increase the efficiency of youth development investment (EPPP, 2010).

The EPPP aims to promote long-term technical excellence in players and financial viability in clubs. In order to achieve this, academies are independently audited and given a category status of one to four, with one being the highest category and receiving the most funding. Ten different factors are considered in the audit grading process, including: productivity rates; training facilities; coaching; education; and welfare provisions. The EPPP will see the Premier League and The FA invest more central income than ever before in youth development programmes across the country (EPPP, 2010).

Building on the success of The Future Game and the established EPPP, the England DNA was introduced in 2014, which is the start point for the creation of a world-class approach to elite player development, leading to successful England teams. It is a statement about the identity and character of England's development teams in both the male (U15s–U21s) and female (U15s–U23s) game. It is also a statement about The FA's fundamental and distinctive characteristics both on and off the pitch, its values and standards of behaviour, and the factors The FA believes are important. It provides a definition of football identity and a structure for all those involved to follow.

The FA considers the England DNA to be ever evolving, although the core values and principles will not change. The FA will be constantly striving to improve every aspect of the DNA. It will evolve to reflect changing trends, latest research and new ideas and inputs. The English game, at all levels, will have a clear vision of what The FA wants to achieve and how it will work. Moreover, England DNA will guide all football education in the country, leading the content and methodology of FA courses and FA continuous professional development (CPD) events.

The current FA strategic priority

The FA has identified the immediate need to prioritise and support the nation's players and coaches in order to ensure the long-term success and health of our game. The recognition of insufficient numbers of high-quality English players, coaches and coach educators in comparison to our European counterparts led to an attempt to reverse these recent trends and formulate a clear, integrated plan across the whole game (professional and grassroots) to positively influence change and raise standards across the coaching workforce. Furthermore, The FA will be setting ambitious coaching targets to be achieved over the next three years, focusing on increasing the numbers of skilled coach educators, which in turn should result in an increased number of highly qualified coaches (The FA Chairman's England Commission Report 2, 2014).

This process entails addressing the major issues in coaching and player development, which includes fundamental questions around what, how, when and where The FA teaches the game. It includes the quality and depth of The FA coach educators communicating the messages of The FA's coaching philosophy. In addition, The FA must ensure we not only qualify coaches, but also encourage them to be 'active' in the game and progress along the coaching pathway. There are also numerous 'active' coaches who are not qualified and The FA has initiated a communications programme to reach these people and move them from unqualified to qualified status. Every effort has been made to increase the number of active and qualified coaches in regional county football associations (excluding the armed forces).

Development of The FA coaching framework

In order to accomplish the vision in the DNA, recognising The FA priorities, a robust infrastructure has been created centred on a modified Coaching Framework. This framework originated following the formation of the European Coaching Framework that detailed the importance of coach education and development, including the need to ensure that the role of coaching was recognised by governments, sport and the wider community. The UK Coaching Framework emerged as a further enhancement of the coaching agenda that builds on previous good work of the Coaching Task Force, Home Country Sports Council and Governing Body of Sport plans. Sports Coach UK conducted an extensive consultation period that led to the formulation of the UK Coaching Framework, which was officially endorsed and launched at the Third UK Coaching Summit in 2008 (Duffy *et al.*, 2011). The UK Coaching Framework provides the reference point for developing a system to move coaching and coach education in the UK towards being a world-leading system. It also aims to deliver many long-held aspirations for coaching. Most importantly, it enhances the quality of the sporting experience at every level for children, players and athletes, and delivers on key government and NGB objectives (Duffy *et al.*, 2011).

The consultation process undertaken during the development of the UK Coaching Framework identified key themes that were built on five strategic action areas (pillars), supported by specific areas of focus, to guide and accelerate coach education and development. The UK Coaching Framework (modified for football) was used to form the foundation of The FA Coaching Strategy (2008–12). The FA refined the pillars through research, organisational and coach feedback to reflect the advances made in coach education and development and introduced the new FA Coaching Strategy (2013–17). The strategy seeks to establish a world-leading coaching programme that produces world-class players. The five pillars are shown in Figure 1.1.

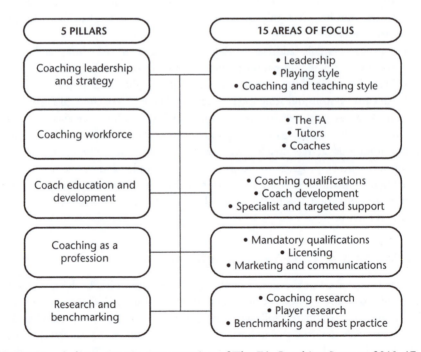

FIGURE 1.1 A diagrammatic representation of The FA Coaching Strategy 2013–17.

Each pillar contains areas of focus that are formed of a series of activities in which specific investigation is conducted in an attempt to establish effectiveness and/or optimum delivery. The five pillars and associated activities have been identified in football and across other major sports as crucial to a successful and coherent coaching framework, enabling for benchmarking across sports. Following discussions with key internal stakeholders, it was agreed that there should be some form of priority to the coaching research programme. It was agreed that priority areas should align with The FA Coaching Strategy, the coaching research strategy, the DNA and should work across the whole game.

Development of The FA coaching research strategy and processes

The coaching research strategy cycle (Figure 1.2) is fundamental in The FA's approach to coaching research and is considered an integral procedure in the foundation and the success of its coach education and development programme. The main aims of The FA's research into coaching are to:

- support the coaching strategy with high-quality, up-to-date, evidence-based research;
- generate and deliver research that is relevant, easily understood and effectively communicated;
- inform and shape policy to assist in the development and improvement of world-class coaches and players;
- provide research that can be practically applied across the whole game.

Furthermore, in the next four years research into coaching will focus on the following areas:

- A research programme to independently (use of external experts in selected fields) measure the effectiveness of coaching.
- A research programme to assess The FA's coach education scheme, coach retention and delivery.
- Internationally benchmark (selected aspects of) The FA's coach education performance.

Previously, the research conducted at The FA was minimal, outsourced to only a few selected researchers and HE institutions and managed as individual projects. Arguably, this was problematic in creating a lack of long-term and unified planning. Therefore, a new philosophy and a strategic approach to the research process was introduced to ensure that research across the various coaching domains had cohesion and a co-ordinated approach. The FA has shown their commitment to this initiative by:

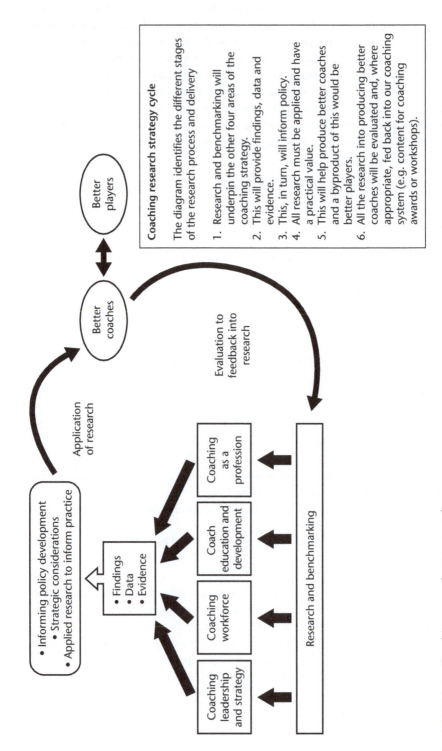

Coaching research strategy cycle

The diagram identifies the different stages of the research process and delivery

1. Research and benchmarking will underpin the other four areas of the coaching strategy.
2. This will provide findings, data and evidence.
3. This, in turn, will inform policy.
4. All research must be applied and have a practical value.
5. This will help produce better coaches and a byproduct of this would be better players.
6. All the research into producing better coaches will be evaluated and, where appropriate, fed back into our coaching system (e.g. content for coaching awards or workshops).

Better players

Better coaches

Evaluation to feedback into research

Application of research

• Informing policy development
• Strategic considerations
• Applied research to inform practice

• Findings
• Data
• Evidence

Coaching leadership and strategy

Coaching workforce

Coach education and development

Coaching as a profession

Research and benchmarking

FIGURE 1. 2   Coaching research strategy cycle.

- introducing the role of Coaching Research Manager, who is responsible for delivering against the coaching strategy and the coaching research strategy, providing the underpinning knowledge of research to inform policy that can be practically applied to support and enhance coach and player development across the whole game;
- increasing the research budget so that additional projects can be conducted every year with the aim to further collaborate with existing and new expert researchers and HE institutions, both nationally and internationally;
- promoting the coaching research strategy to illustrate how The FA can use research to demonstrate impact and to bring about a real change in coach education and development, thus supporting a cultural shift in how research is perceived and conducted by an NGB.

The role of the Coaching Research Manager is centred on four key areas: relationships, communication, support and project management. The following sections outline the role and illustrate the new procedures that have been adopted by The FA.

Relationships

The role includes establishing working relationships with internal FA staff and external bodies, such as the Premier League, Football League, the Professional Footballers' Association (PFA), professional football clubs, the League Managers Association (LMA), the Professional Football Coaches Association (PFCA), higher and further education (FE) specialist providers, UEFA and FIFA, and other footballing research bodies. Developing relationships with independent researchers and HE is an important factor within the role. Anecdotal evidence suggests that many NGBs could be considered 'anti-intellectual' in their approach to independent research and are suspicious of academic theory being integrated and allowed to drive their everyday activity. It could be said that NGBs are uncomfortable at having their processes and procedures evaluated and being advised of what to do by 'academics'. Several factors lead to this problem, including culture, the confidential and sensitive nature of information and possible perceptions when flaws in current practice are identified. Such issues could make them relatively difficult to work with, making it a challenge for any researcher or HE institution.

Having said that, the role recognises that NGBs can be key stakeholders in the research process, benefiting themselves and the wider community. They can provide access to national and international performers (players/athletes; coaches; coach educators) to ensure that the research has participants of the highest quality. They can provide funding to support research on topics of greatest benefit to themselves, providing evidence-based information to inform their practices. Moreover, working on research projects with NGBs is a marker of esteem for researchers and HE institutions, while the external funding provided for such projects enables them to achieve one of their key performance indicators. HE and expert researchers have a lot to offer the sporting community in terms of providing theoretical and (in some cases) practical expertise, structured rationales, an independent perspective based on years of study in the relevant field and a balance of the inclusion of research to underpin policy and practice (used in an advisory capacity). Therefore, in essence, both parties should appreciate the value of research collaboration, and it is the role of the Coaching Research Manager to develop these collaborative relationships.

Communication

There are a number of communication channels and opportunities related to this programme of work and it is vital to establish communication links with football partners and HE/FE specialist providers, as well as other experts in the field. In some cases (not all), part of the role includes the translation of the research report from the academic writing into a 'user friendly' format highlighting key information, the benefit to The FA and what it means for coach education and development across the whole game. Dissemination of information to various coaching groups is important, as it brings the research project to life and provides the opportunity for detailed questions to be asked. The role includes producing articles for The FA magazine *The Boot Room* and posting research articles on the coaching library (an internal resource bank) where possible. As part of our agreement with HE, the research is released for publications, conferences, book chapters and various academic resources, on the proviso that all sensitive information be either removed or discussed as to how it is best presented.

Support

Part of the role includes the identification of internal staff for research and development projects and to support individuals to develop abstracts, methodologies and reports. Support is also given to external coaching researchers who can demonstrate that their area of investigation aligns with our coaching strategy and warrants FA involvement and guidance.

Project management

A major role is project management, which includes devising a coaching research project procedure for placing short- (six months), medium- (6–12 months) and long-term (18+ months) projects in HE, FE and other specialist providers, ensuring that the specific project briefs are being followed and deadlines are met. No commissioned coaching research is 'ad hoc', so for consistency and clarity *all* projects follow the same process in design and application.

The project process shown in Figure 1.3 follows the 11 steps below:

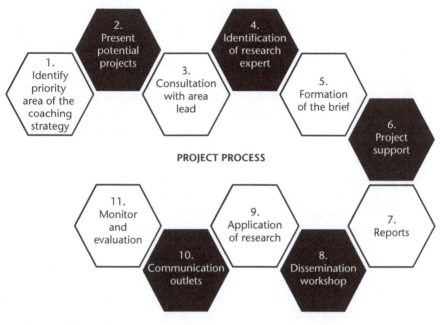

FIGURE 1.3   The project process.

1.   When deciding a project, consideration is given to the priority area in relation to the coaching strategy and the DNA. A number of factors influence the priority list (key stakeholder involvement; political importance; current issues; FA initiatives, etc.) and careful attention is paid to the five potential projects per year. Every effort is made to ensure that there's a balance of research across the whole game.
2.   These five potential projects are then presented to the Education Group; the rationale is provided and discussed before it is either accepted or rejected by the group, based on the factors highlighted in step 1.
3.   Accepted projects are followed by consultation with the area lead. During this meeting, it is essential to ascertain:
   •   the aims and purpose of the research;
   •   how the proposed research aligns with the coaching strategy, coaching research strategy and the DNA, and the overall benefit to the organisation;
   •   the intended use of the final report and recommendations (policy – acquiring additional funding, etc.; course content; coach/tutor training and CPD, etc.);
   •   logistics: how are we going to support the researcher in terms of access to key people (internal and external); participants required; and length of the study;
   •   a logic modelling procedure to establish the research question(s) by identifying the underlying assumptions of the specific area, the intended planned work, potential outcomes and how the impact of the research can be demonstrated.

This meeting is vital as it not only shapes the intended research, but also helps with obtaining the 'buy-in' of the area lead. Furthermore, it gives them an appreciation of the planning and operational aspect of the research process, together with an understanding of what would be required for short-, medium- and long-term projects, depending on the focus and why the research is needed.

4.   For credibility and to guarantee the independent nature of the research, a researcher is identified at this stage based on their expertise in the particular field and *not* determined by the institution that they are attached to. The coaching research expert identification criteria include some of the following:

   * consideration is made on his or her professional achievements and credentials to establish whether they are actually an expert in their field.
   * a high degree of experience (both length and breadth), education and authority in their field.
   * experience working in projects similar to those for which they are required.
   * his or her educational achievements should be consistent with those of other professionals in their field.
   * ideally, an expert has significant real-world experience in the field for which they consult.
   * consultation made with previous employers, colleagues and clients about the expert's work ethic, quality of work and ability to complete projects on time.
   * review of his or her publication record as a history of publication in industry magazines or peer-reviewed journals is typically a strong indication of an expert's competency and expertise.
   * determination of whether his or her services are affordable and establishing if they are capable of meeting deadlines and will be available for consultation on the project.

5.   The project brief is then constructed, detailing deadline dates and headings to be included in the proposal, interim and final reports. For legal purposes, it is at this stage that the researcher is sent The FA service provider agreement/ contract. No projects are allowed to commence until this has been agreed and signed.

6.   Support is given (via one-to-one visits every two months and regular email and telephone contact) from The FA and related staff and the researchers are also given access to key internal FA staff if required.

7.   The researchers are required to provide both an interim and a final report.

8.   Two to four weeks after the final report has been received, it is then circulated internally to a group of key staff and a dissemination workshop (at the discretion of The FA) usually takes place, whereby the researchers present their findings to a group.

9.   The Education Group then decides the application of the research. A key aspect of the strategy cycle (Figure 1.2) is the application and translation of the findings from the research process. To ensure that there is a smooth translation,

with the information going to the area for which it was intended, the commissioned research is submitted in the form of a report to an Education Group (policy-makers). They have the authority to certify that recommendations from the research are applied to specific areas, such as policy development, strategy, course content, course delivery or the DNA.

10. Communication outlets are the various places where the findings of the project reports can be disseminated. It is only intended that each report will go to a selected group with a specific interest in the findings. An example of these include:

- internal – Coach Education Forum, heads of departments, *Boot Room* magazine, Research and Innovation Update newsletter, coaching library, contribution to CPD activities, course content;
- professional game – Premier League, Football League, LMA, PFA;
- national game – county football associations, specialist projects (Skills Programme), women's game;
- education – HE/FE journal articles, book chapters, conferences, course content;
- other bodies – European Football Associations, sport NGBs, Sports Coach UK, Sport England, UK Sport, selected media.

11. This process is monitored and evaluated every year to assess its effectiveness.

By having a Coaching Research Manager in place, The FA has taken the responsibility and commitment to investigate key components of the coaching system and initiate innovative, football-specific research. This highlights the importance of the role and its value to the coach education and development programme, which is pivotal to the coaching strategy in an attempt to produce a first-class coaching workforce.

The FA is determined that coaching research makes a much greater impact on policy and practice within coach education and development across the whole game. The FA coaching research strategy forms part of the overall approach to research and innovation. It complements The FA Coaching Strategy and specifically addresses knowledge about coach education and development, highlighting how coaches, coach educators and players can benefit from research, and with a carefully constructed programme of investigation illustrates how The FA can use research to demonstrate impact and to bring about a positive change in coach education and development.

The FA context: from present to future

The main aim of The FA's coach education and development programme must be clearly connected to the context and requirements of the coach. With that in mind, several objectives of the coach education programme are outlined, notably introducing reflective practice and pedagogical theory and evidence, as it is thought that this will stimulate informed critical debate. Therefore, there is a need to employ tutors or guest speakers who can meaningfully communicate complex ideas to coaches. It is hoped that the further development of innovative learning and assessment environments will lead to formal, informal and non-formal learning occurring, which facilitates transfer from theory to practice within their particular environment, as coaches often develop through constructing their learning through informal situations (Cassidy *et al.*, 2009; Loyens *et al.*, 2007).

Currently, there is an excellent opportunity to work with professional clubs to identify players who are at the end of their careers or are being released to provide a future career pathway in coaching. The FA is committed to identifying and developing talented English coaches. There is also a requirement for more specialist mentoring and support programmes designed to assist female coaches and those who work with ethnic minority and disabled player groups. Recent successful initiatives have included The FA Youth Coach Educators (FAYCE's) programme, whereby 18 coach educators provide support to academy coaches of professional clubs on a regional basis. In addition, The FA Club Mentoring programme is a major investment in the grassroots game and offers on-the-ground support to FA Charter Standard clubs and coaches.

The FA is also dedicated to ensuring that a comprehensive CPD programme is in place to support all these areas and recognise its value and importance. This structured, enhanced CPD programme is an important requirement of all FA and UEFA awards and is required to maintain coaching awards and to improve standards of The FA's coach education and development programme.

Critical questions for NGBs

1. How can you start to implement coaching research into your organisation? What would you need to consider first? Who would you need to influence?
2. How would you ensure that coaching research is used as a functional resource unit that underpins and provides up-to-date, evidence-based rationales for what you do and why?
3. Do you have a research strategy for the next four years?
4. How can/have you made that transfer from research to policy to practice?
5. How do you manage the research projects when sensitive and confidential information is discussed?
6. Is your institution in a position to embrace a cultural change to aid a collaborative research process with HE?

References

Cassidy, T., Jones, R. & Potrac, P. (2009). *Understanding sports coaching: the social, cultural and pedagogical foundations of coaching practice*, 2nd edn. London: Routledge.

Duffy, P., Hartley, H., Bales, J., Crespo, M., Dick, F., Vardhan, D., Nordmann, L. & Curado, J. (2011). Sport coaching as a 'profession': challenges and future directions. *International Journal of Coaching Science*, 5 (2), 93–123.

Elite Player Performance Plan (EPPP) (2010). Premier League Youth Development. Available: www.premierleague.com/content/premierleague/en-gb/youth/elite-player-performance-plan.html, last accessed 10 May 2015.

FA Chairman's England Commission Report 2, The (2014). Available: www.sportsthinktank.com/uploads/the-fa-fa-chairmans-england-commission-report-2-october-2014.pdf, last accessed 10 May 2015.

Future Game, The (2010). Available: www.thefa.com/st-georges-park/discover/coaching/the-future-game, last accessed 10 May 2015.

Loyens, S.M.M., Rikers, R.M.J.P. & Schmidt, H.G. (2007). Students' conceptions of distinct constructivist assumptions. *European Journal of Psychology of Education*, 22 (2), 179–199.

PART I

Contextual issues

2

BENCHMARKING SPORT COACH EDUCATION AND DEVELOPMENT

Using programme theories to examine and evolve current practice

Julian North

Introduction

This chapter provides a new perspective on benchmarking coach education and development based on the work of Duffy *et al.* (2012). Benchmarking compares principles, processes and practices to other leading experts and organisations. Thus, applied to football, benchmarking provides a tool, for example, for national associations such as The English Football Association (The FA) to understand how its coach education and development principles, processes and practices compare to the best in the world. In Europe obvious countries for comparative benchmarking analysis include Belgium, Germany, the Netherlands and Spain. Benchmarking is important because it provides information both on good and bad practices of the leading footballing nations, and shows the strengths and weaknesses of the focus country. This information can be used to inform coaching system development and improvement which should in turn, *ceteris paribus*, lead to better coaching, improved player experiences and increased game performance.

Existing research

Although there are a number of academic resources available to researchers and practitioners interested in the comparative aspects of sport policy (e.g. Houlihan, 1997), there is less available to those wishing to explore the comparative aspects of coach education and development. A recent search suggests there are two main strands of activity to inform this area: *descriptive* research, i.e. descriptive of coach education and development; and *prescriptive* policy and practice resources, i.e. sets out a position to guide thinking on coach education and development.

First, the descriptive work. Although based largely on practitioner experience (rather than systematic empirical research), important mention should be given to

Sue Campbell, whose 1993 'Coach education around the world' article first highlighted the importance of thinking about the comparative aspects of coach education and development (Campbell, 1993). Since then, there appears to have been only one academic international comparative study of football coach education (Nash, 2003), and this of only relatively limited scope. There has been comparative work on football player development which has implications for coach education and development (e.g. Holt, 2002; Fisher & Dean, 1998; Ford *et al.*, 2012). There has been comparative sport federation-commissioned and consultant-delivered research on coach education and development in rugby union (Studd & Gittus, 2013). There has been comparative sport federation-generated research on coach education and development in tennis (Crespo *et al.*, 2005a, 2005b; Zmajic, 2011). Finally, colleagues at Leeds Beckett University have also undertaken international comparative work focused on international coach education programme evaluation (Muir *et al.*, 2012).

Second, the prescriptive work. To our knowledge there is only one internationally supported framework that provides prescriptive guidance on coach education and development. The International Council for Coaching Excellence (ICCE) has developed the *International Sport Coaching Framework* (ISCF) (ICCE *et al.*, 2013). The ISCF offers generic ideas on coaching roles, coaching knowledge and competence, coach education and development, and qualification frameworks which can be applied by individual countries and sports. The ICCE has also been working on similar guidance for coach developers through the International Coach Developer Framework (ICDF) (ICCE *et al.*, 2014).

This research work and policy guidance has been very useful for providing some early approaches and insight into comparative coaching and coach development across different sporting nations. However, it is limited for current purposes because it does not provide explicit benchmarking/comparative tools.

FA case study research: key concepts

The FA work and the choice of underpinning framework

In early 2012 The FA asked Leeds Beckett University (formerly Leeds Metropolitan University) to benchmark the English approach to football coach education and development against the principles, policies, programmes and practices in France, Germany, Italy, the Netherlands and Spain. Benchmarking was also undertaken against five leading sports in the UK: cricket, cycling, golf, rowing and rugby union.

The principal researcher on the project was Professor Pat Duffy – a great innovator and leader in sport coaching policy and practice, friend and colleague, and sadly no longer with us. The research was written up in the report 'Benchmarking coach education and development' (Duffy *et al.*, 2012). At the time the research was commissioned, the author of this chapter was exploring the philosophy and social theory of critical realism (CR) to describe, explain and change sport coaching practice. The first parts of this CR project have been published in North (2013a, 2013b).

One application of CR ideas is the evaluation methodology 'realist evaluation', outlined in Pawson and Tilley (1997) and supplemented by a number of previous and subsequent resources (e.g. Pawson, 1989, 2006, 2013; Pawson & Tilley, 2004). Professor Duffy – assisted by the research team – believed there to be considerable merit in realist evaluation to underpin coach education and development benchmarking work in an area that, as we have noted, is not rich in extant resources.

Because of their explicit philosophical underpinnings, CR and realist evaluation are not easy to grasp on first read. However, with sustained engagement it becomes apparent they provide a robust grounding for researchers, and ultimately lead to a very useful set of practical tools for research which help to negotiate and capture the complexities of the social world (e.g. sport, sport coaching, sport education and development). The interested reader is encouraged to start with the work of Pawson cited above, but the work extends beyond this into philosophy (e.g. Collier, 1994), psychology (e.g. Martin *et al.*, 2003) and sociology (e.g. Archer, 1995; Sayer, 2000; Elder-Vass, 2010), among other areas and disciplines.

Realist evaluation and programme theories

Realist evaluation is specifically concerned with programmes – such as coach education and development programmes. Realist evaluation thinks of programmes as sets of *programme theories*. Programme theories are ideas about how and why particular areas of social life work, and thus how and why particular goals or *outcomes* can be achieved in these areas. If we know how and why something works, then we can use this knowledge to make things happen or to effect change:

> Programmes are shaped by a vision of change and they succeed or fail according to the veracity of that vision.
>
> *(Pawson & Tilley, 2004: p. 2)*

For example, if our goal is to better educate and develop football coaches, realist evaluation focuses on how this might be achieved (e.g. providing coaches with the appropriate knowledge and experiences), and why programme developers think it will work or not (e.g. because research and experience suggest that effective quality coaches have appropriate levels of knowledge and experience to inform their reasoning and strategising).

Realist evaluation suggests that programmes are *embedded*, that is, situated in a complex configuration of interacting layers related to *individual* capacities, *interpersonal relationships*, *institutions* and wider *socio-cultural* systems. In a coach education and development context this might relate to individual coach educators/ developers and their student coaches; their interpersonal relations, relations with important others, clubs and other social institutions such as the family; and socio-cultural systems such as governing body administration, the media, etc.

Embeddedness has implications for programme design, implementation and evaluation which eschews simple solutions. In its place it suggests complexity and multiple determination. For example, a simple programme theory may posit that the provision of information to football coaches on player hydration may lead to improved coaching practices in this area and, with this, potentially improved player performance. A realist evaluation programme theory would recognise that the success of the programme is contingent on a myriad of factors including those offered, but not exhausted, by this simple approach.

To continue the example: the research underpinning the workshop may be flawed (socio-cultural system). The coach may not be in the mood to be talked at for an hour about hydration because she has had a bad day at work (individual). The coach educator's information may be contradicted by other information the coach has read, or by an influential peer (interpersonal relationships). The coach's club may have a specific hydration policy (institutional). The players may not be willing to accept the coach's hydration advice because she does not command the authority or respect to induce player behavioural change (interpersonal relationships).

This level of complexity and multiple determination is seen as a characteristic of all programmes. Therefore, realist evaluators do not ask questions such as 'does the programme work or not work' as if there is some definitive conclusion. They ask instead 'what works, for whom, in what conditions, and why'?

> Programmes are products of the foresight of policy-makers. Their fate though ultimately always depends on the imagination of practitioners and participants. Rarely do these visions fully coincide. Interventions never work indefinitely, in the same way and in all circumstances, or for all people.
>
> *(Pawson & Tilley, 2004: p. 3)*

Thus, programme theories and the *mechanisms* that underpin them are always proposed and judged in particular *contexts*. What might work in one context may fail in another, and may even produce counter-productive or perverse effects.

For realist evaluators, then, policy-makers, practitioners and researchers have to understand how and why their particular goals or outcomes (O), are achieved by particular mechanisms (M), in particular contexts (C). Realist evaluators talk about CMO configurations being the basis for programme theory development and evaluation, including in benchmarking and comparative activities.

Using realist evaluation to benchmark coach education and development

There is a great deal more depth and complexity to the realist evaluation methodology than suggested above (the interested reader can refer back to the texts already mentioned). The approach proposed by Duffy *et al.* (2012) simplifies the realist evaluation approach to establishing a basic framework to undertake benchmarking activities in football coach education and development across five European countries and five top UK sports. The more complex realist evaluation methodology was therefore adopted and adapted to meet the specific needs of the client and the task. The approach draws on the two tools highlighted above – embeddedness and programme theories expressed through CMO relationships.

Embeddedness

Duffy *et al.* (2012) adopt the embedded framework proposed by realistic evaluation but extend it to incorporate 'the game', which is obviously a central component in the analysis of football (Figure 2.1).

The game provides the rules, participation context, traditions and cultures which are so important to the other layers within the football system. For Duffy *et al.* (2012) the individual layer concerns players and coaches, and might also be extended to important individual others such as club officials and coach educators

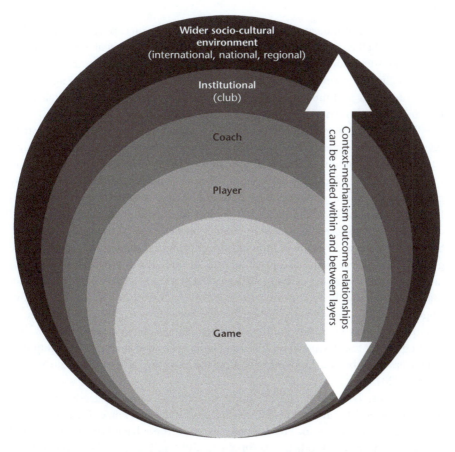

FIGURE 2.1   Embeddedness of sport coaching and coach education and development.

and developers. The interpersonal layer concerns the interaction between these stakeholders. The institutional layer concerns most notably the clubs where most coach–player interaction takes places, and is also increasingly an important site for coach education and development (North *et al.*, 2015b). The socio-cultural system is captured through reference to wider international, national and regional football and non-football systems.

For each layer, programme theories are expressed through CMO relationships

At each layer of the embedded ecology, Duffy *et al.* (2012) provide a set of programme theories expressed through CMO relationships that provide a basis for undertaking benchmarking analysis of national coach education and development systems.

The game

An appreciation of the game and the way it is played is increasingly recognised in modern football coach education (North *et al.*, 2015b). Duffy *et al.* (2012) contrast the unique social and cultural environment that has shaped the game in England with benchmark countries. For example, as inventor of the game, England has been subject to a number of important historical, structural and cultural forces which continue to shape how the game is viewed and played.

Wilson (2010) provides an overview: the game's origins as an amateur sport in the public school system led to an emphasis on mental strength, pluck and physical stamina over technique and tactical innovation. When England were the best in the world (1900–10) these were strengths that won them games – winning many games in the last few minutes. There were innovative technical/tactical coaches in England, but because of the (amateur) distrust of coaching most of them moved overseas to set up successful systems in other countries – the Netherlands, Germany, Spain, etc. There is a culture of individualism in England which also permeates the game – the English blame bad performances on individuals (coaches and players) rather than on teams and systems. Wilson (2010) suggests further: as inventors of the game there has been a historical arrogance, conservatism and insularity about English football – 'we invented it therefore we know how to play it; we don't need to look at other systems; we don't need others telling us how to play'. This has had a lasting legacy for playing styles, coaching behaviours and spectator consumption, which has long been a hindrance for England in terms of national team success (Wilson, 2010).

In contrast, Duffy *et al.* (2012) point to different contextual conditions and mechanisms which have led to different playing styles in France, Germany, Italy, the Netherlands and Spain. For example, in Spain there have been two historical influences on Spanish football – 'la furia' (the fury) and 'toques' (soft and/or short touches) (North *et al.*, 2015a). These two influences have competed for dominant

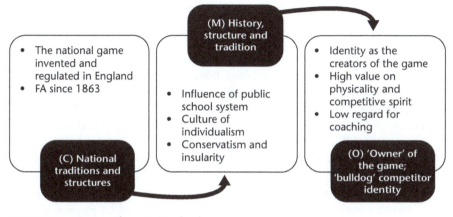

FIGURE 2.2   Game culture in England.

position since the early development of Spanish football but were argued to be in ideal balance during the recent successful period. This has also come to be known as 'silk and steel' or more commonly as 'tiki-taka'.

'La furia' is associated with physicality, aggression, bravery, passion, virility and honour, and is linked to influences from the British game, the Basque region and the idealised Spaniard under Franco (it has also been referred to as 'the bull'). Recent Spanish successes were built as much on defensive parsimony as attacking flair. 'Toques' is associated with short passing, speed, technique, control/ domination of possession, continuous movement, use of space, intelligence, creativity and flair which emerged domestically (the 'Mediterranean style'), from South America (overseas tours, Menotti), Hungary and from the Dutch ('total football') (it has also been referred to as 'the bull-fighter').

From an English perspective, a benchmarking approach which emphasises programme theories and CMO relationships illustrates that it is far from straightforward to change ideas about the game and playing style, for example, through DNA approaches (The Football Association, 2015), to establish a context for future performance improvements. Any DNA approach has to understand how the outcome (a playing style which gives a greater chance of competitive success) is linked to the context and its historical, social and cultural mechanisms.

The player (and player development)

The characteristics of the player and player development approaches are also seen as fundamentally linked to football coach education and development (North *et al.*, 2014). Duffy *et al.* (2012) contrast England's 'player/player development level' with major European footballing nations using CMO configurations. It is interesting that unlike 'the game', they compare the English proposals for player development moving forward as laid out in *The Future Game* (FA Learning, 2010), rather than some assessment of what English provision is actually like at this level. This suggests an interesting benchmarking twist between 'actual' and 'proposed' programme theories, as well as those between countries. All good programme evaluators know that what is written in policy and programme documentation is seldom what occurs at ground level (Pawson & Tilley, 1997). Benchmarkers beware!

For sake of consistency between layers, the analysis offered here will attempt to capture something of the 'what is' rather than the 'what should be' in England (while recognising that things may have changed recently). This will then be compared with the French system, drawing on the work of North *et al.* (2014, 2015a).

Historically, English player development, typically taking place in community clubs and club development centres and academies, has osmosed ideas about the game into its player development philosophy and approach. Thus, the emphasis on physique and competitiveness at the senior level has translated into player development practices. Scouts tend to select youngsters based on physical size and current performance rather than future potential. There is an emphasis on winning rather than development in clubs at all levels – which leads to very different development experiences and coaching. Competition between pro clubs means that *de facto* selection starts at a very young age – around 5–8 years. This has led to players who perform well in younger age groups, but generally fade as they move towards the senior team and international level as early discriminating factors start to even out (as competitor players mature, gain other types of developmental experiences).

In France, a different set of contextual conditions, mechanisms and outcomes have been observed around player development. In France there has been a greater emphasis on beauty, technique, precision and patience in playing style (North *et al.*, 2014). This has led to a much more patient approach to player development, with youngsters not formally selected to club academies until 12 years of age. There is also a much more individualised approach to coaching, using personal and team challenges often in game situations, to develop technical skills and game understanding.

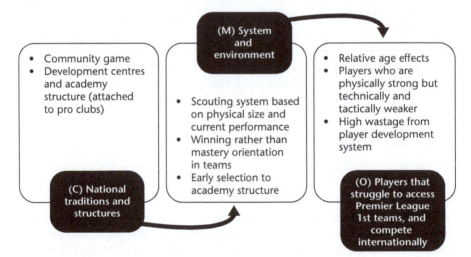

FIGURE 2.3 Player development in the English game.

From an English perspective, the French system provides an example of another development model, one where patience and individualisation are clearly important mechanisms in the development of players. The English system appears to have evolved considerably in recent years, with a new approach to player development (The Football Association, 2015; FA Learning, 2010), coach education concerning the 'youth modules' and the Premier League's *Elite Player Performance Plan* (Premier League, 2011). It is of course difficult to conclude definitively on the state of the English game, but that is not our main purpose here. This is to show the usefulness of a programme theory benchmarking approach.

The coach

An understanding of coaching, coaching characteristics, expertise and excellence is of course very important to developing high-quality coach education and development. Duffy *et al.* (2012) contrast England's 'coaching level' with major European footballing nations using CMO configurations. Again, Duffy *et al.* adopt a forward-looking approach as laid out in *The Future Game* (FA Learning, 2010), rather than providing an assessment of what English coaching provision is actually like. Again I will try to capture something of the 'what is' (although recognising that the picture is changing and subject to various interventions already mentioned), before comparing it with a benchmark European country.

The institutional context for coaching in England is largely the same as/ synonymous with player development, with most activity occurring in community clubs, and development centres and academies connected to pro clubs (Figure 2.4). Historically, the coach has been central to player development activities, with environments more 'coach centred' than 'player centred' (e.g. Potrac *et al.*, 2002; Wilson, 2010; Cushion & Jones, 2006). One result of this has been a focus on team development and performance rather than a focus on individual development (already referred to in the player section, showing the interrelation of mechanisms between layers).

Coaching in England has also tended to focus on the replication of existing 'traditional' coaching knowledge rather than referring to sports science research (Williams & Hodges, 2005) or searching for good practice from elsewhere (Wilson, 2010). This has often led to the overuse of traditional rigid skills-drills training approaches abstracted from the actual playing of the game, which has been argued to undermine English players' technical and tactical development (Cushion *et al.*, 2012).

In the Netherlands, a very different set of coaching practices has emerged (North *et al.*, 2014). The Dutch place considerable socio-cultural importance on individualism, which permeates attitudes to coaching. The coaches work individually with the players to develop their 4Zs (4Ss in English) – self-regulation, self-initiative, self-reliance and self-development. There is also a considerable emphasis in Dutch coaching on 'the game as the teacher'. All player development aspects – physical, psychological, social, technical and tactical characteristics – are

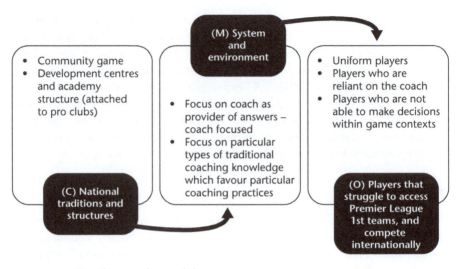

FIGURE 2.4   Coaching in the English game.

developed as much as possible with reference to authentic game experiences. This, it is suggested, leads to the development of players who take responsibility and are capable of making decisions on and off the field. This again provides interesting ideas for the English game – what is the role of the coach? How is training being organised, and is it optimal for player development?

Implications for practitioners

Duffy *et al.* (2012) work through each of the remaining layers – institutional and wider socio-cultural – to highlight some important CMO relationships which cast light on the English coach education and development system compared to benchmark countries and sports. As noted in the introduction, governing bodies like The FA can use this information to understand the strengths and weaknesses of their systems using a programme theories approach understood as layers of CMOs in an embedded system.

The benchmarking illustrated above does not seek to provide a current state of the nation view on English football and how it compares to other major European football nations and major sports. What it does instead, using a number of research and practitioner-based examples, is provide a new way of thinking about programmes, i.e. as programme theories, how they are layered into different component parts from the game to the wider environment. At each layer, CMO relationships can be identified which help practitioners think more clearly about how and why their programmes work in specific contexts, how they can be meaningfully compared to other benchmark nations, and what it is possible to change, and what it is not.

There are a number of important lessons from this approach. The need to understand the relationship between context and mechanism in search of particular outcomes warns against the uncritical borrowing of 'good practice' ideas from other contexts (North *et al.*, 2014). There is now a great deal of cross-national sharing of footballing ideas (North *et al.*, 2015b), but football associations, system architects and coaches need to be careful when applying ideas from one context to another. This leads to a wider point about developing programmes and system change. If national football associations wish to effect change, this must be grounded in a clear understanding of context, and how programmes and their mechanisms can be used to generate desired outcomes. This suggests the clever use of top-down programmatic approaches which empower coach developers, academy managers and coaches to develop and use their knowledge and skills to achieve goals at the programme/local level.

Critical questions

1. What are coach education and development programmes? Are they homogeneous 'lumps' of programme ideas, or are they made of many interacting parts?
2. How does the success or failure of coach education and development programmes relate to context? Do all programme ideas work in all contexts?
3. How can we understand coach education and development programmes as programme theories, and CMO relationships in an embedded ecology? What do your programme theories look like? How do they change by level?
4. How can we understand and compare our coach education and development programme with those that exist in other countries and sports? What ideas can we borrow and apply? What ideas will be more difficult to implement?

References

Archer, M. (1995). *Realist social theory: the morphogenetic approach*. Cambridge: Cambridge University Press.

Campbell, S. (1993). Coach education around the world. *Sports Science Review*, 2, 62–74.

Collier, A. (1994). *Critical realism*. London: Verso.

Crespo, M., Reid, M., McInerney, P. & Miley, D. (2005a). Tennis coaches education: comparison of tutor-contact hours worldwide. *Coaching & Sport Science Review*, 37, 12–13.

Crespo, M., Reid, M. & Miley, D. (2005b). Tennis coaches education: a worldwide perspective. *Coaching & Sport Science Review*, 35, 11–13.

Cushion, C.J. & Jones, R.L. (2006). Power, discourse, and symbolic violence in professional youth soccer: the case of Albion Football Club. *Sociology of Sport Journal*, 23, 142–161.

Cushion, C.J., Ford, P. & Williams, A.M. (2012). Coach behaviours and practice structures in youth soccer: implications for talent development. *Journal of Sports Sciences*, 30, 1631–1641.

Duffy, P., Patterson, L., North, J., Lara-Bercial, S. & Rongen, F. (2012). *Benchmarking coach education and development: an interim research report for The Football Association*. Leeds: Leeds Metropolitan University.

Elder-Vass, D. (2010). *The causal power of social structures: emergence, structure and agency*. Cambridge: Cambridge University Press.

FA Learning (2010). *The future game*. London: FA Learning.

Fisher, R. & Dean, M. (1998). A comparative study of the development of elite young soccer players in England and Belgium. *Journal of Comparative Physical Education & Sport*, 20, 44–51.

Football Association, The (2015). *England DNA*. Burton Upon Trent: The Football Association.

Ford, P.R., Carling, C., Garces, M., Marques, M., Miguel, C., Farrant, A., Stenling, A., Moreno, J., Le Gall, F., Holmström, S., Salmela, J.H. & Williams, M. (2012). The developmental activities of elite soccer players aged under-16 years from Brazil, England, France, Ghana, Mexico, Portugal and Sweden. *Journal of Sports Sciences*, 30, 1653–1663.

Holt, N.L. (2002). A comparison of the soccer talent development systems in England and Canada. *European Physical Education Review*, 8, 270–285.

Houlihan, B. (1997). *Sport, policy and politics: a comparative approach*. London: Routledge.

ICCE, ASOIF & LMU (2013). *International sport coaching framework v1.2*. Champaign, IL: Human Kinetics.

ICCE, ASOIF & LMU (2014). *International coach developer framework v1.1*. Leeds: ICCE.

Martin, J., Sugarman, J. & Thompson, J. (2003). *Psychology and the question of agency*. Albany, NY: State University of New York Press.

Muir, B., Richards, I., Duffy, P., North, J. & Boocock, E. (2012). *Evaluation of the International Community Coach Education Systems (ICES)*. Leeds: Leeds Metropolitan University.

Nash, C. (2003). Coaching effectiveness and coach education programmes: perceptions of Scottish and US coaches. *International Sports Studies*, 25, 21–31.

North, J. (2013a). A critical realist approach to theorising coaching practice. In Potrac, P., Gilbert, W.D. & Dennison, J. (eds), *The Routledge handbook of sports coaching*. London: Routledge.

North, J. (2013b). Philosophical underpinnings of coaching practice research. *Quest*, 65, 278–299.

North, J., Lara-Bercial, S., Morgan, G. & Rongen, F. (2014). *The identification of good practice principles to inform player development and coaching in European youth football: a literature review and expert interviews in Belgium, England, France, Germany, Italy, the Netherlands, and Spain in the performance pathway. A research report for UEFA*. Leeds: Research Institute for Sport, Physical Activity and Leisure, Leeds Beckett University.

North, J., Lara-Bercial, S., Patterson, L., Rongen, F. & Duffy, P. (2015a). *Benchmarking leadership and game culture in English and Spanish football and New Zealand rugby union: a research report for the Football Association*. Leeds: Research Institute for Sport, Physical Activity and Leisure, Leeds Beckett University.

North, J., Piggott, D., Lyle, J., Lara-Bercial, S., Muir, B., Petrovic, L., Norman, L., Abraham, A. & Shaw, W. (2015b). *Research study on the UEFA Coaching Convention: a research report for UEFA*. Leeds: Research Institute for Sport, Physical Activity and Leisure, Leeds Beckett University.

Pawson, R. (1989). *A measure for measures: a manifesto for empirical sociology*. London: Routledge.

Pawson, R. (2006). *Evidence based policy: a realist perspective*. London: Sage.

Pawson, R. (2013). *The science of evaluation: a realist manifesto*. London: Sage.

Pawson, R. & Tilley, N. (1997). *Realistic evaluation*. London: Sage.

Pawson, R. & Tilley, N. (2004). *Realist evaluation*. London: British Cabinet Office.

Potrac, P., Jones, R.L. & Armour, K. (2002). 'It's all about getting respect': the coaching behaviors of an expert English soccer coach. *Sport, Education and Society*, 7, 183–202.

Premier League (2011). *Elite player performance plan*. London: Premier League.

Sayer, A. (2000). *Realism and social science*. London: Sage.

Studd, S. & Gittus, B. (2013). *Coach education in rugby union: global comparative study*. Dublin: International Rugby Board and European Observatoire of Sport and Employment.

Williams, A.M. & Hodges, N.J. (2005). Practice, instruction and skill acquisition in soccer: challenging tradition. *Journal of Sports Sciences*, 23, 637–650.

Wilson, J. (2010). *The anatomy of England*. London: Orion Books.

Zmajic, H. (2011). Coach education systems in Europe: a competencies comparison. *Coaching & Sport Science Review (Spanish Version)*, 19, 7–9.

3

CPD PROVISION FOR THE FOOTBALL COACHING WORKFORCE

What can we learn from other professional fields and what are the implications?

Kathleen Armour, Mark Griffiths and Alexander De Lyon

Introduction

One of the key characteristics of any recognised profession is practitioners who have both the right and the responsibility to engage in appropriate and effective career-long professional learning (Brunetti, 1998). The reason for this requirement is clear: a profession exists to serve its clients, and a professional practitioner should be able to draw upon best knowledge at any given time to serve clients effectively.

As described in much of the coaching research, football coaches report that their formal accreditation and continuing professional development (CPD) experiences are often negative (e.g. Nelson & Cushion, 2006). In particular, coaches have criticised the prescriptive nature of coaching courses, the tendency to provide too much information at one time, and content that appears to be irrelevant to their practice contexts (Chesterfield *et al.*, 2010; Lemyre *et al.*, 2007; Jones *et al.*, 2003). Research literature on coaching as a profession is growing, but research focusing specifically on the professional development of football coaches is notably scarce.

A key critique identified in research conducted with football coaches is that CPD courses lack relevance in both content and design. Nash (2003), for example, argues that CPD tends to focus on the 'what' of coaching rather than the 'how', leading to an over-reliance on hypothetical and idealised situations. A UK-based study by Chesterfield *et al.* (2010), entitled '"Studentship" and "impression management" in an advanced soccer coach education award', illustrates the issue. The research investigated the views of six coaches who had recently completed the UEFA 'A' Coaching Licence. The participants reported that they actively rejected the majority of coaching practices promoted by the course tutors because what was taught clashed with their personal experiences of 'what works' and was unsuited to the needs of their football clubs. An additional concern is the finding that in a bid to become certified, coaches openly admitted to 'staging a performance' by mimicking the behaviours of the course tutors in order to pass the observed assessments. This can be characterised as a 'strategic passing' strategy and is the antithesis of learning.

It is important to note that these findings are not restricted to the UK, but appear to reflect wider findings about the education of football coaches. Hammond and Perry's (2005) study focused on 'A multi-dimensional assessment of soccer coaching course effectiveness', and investigated two junior licence coaching courses conducted in New South Wales, Australia. While modules within these courses were designed to address the 'how' of coaching – i.e. the craft or pedagogical practices – the study indicated that this was overlooked in favour of more technical and procedural knowledge. The authors contend that future research should address the instructional practices used by coach educators when attempting to convey anything beyond technical information. Nash (2002, 2003) found similar results when investigating the perceptions of football coaches who had attended education courses in the USA and Scotland. Across both nations, the overwhelming response of coaches to CPD was negative. For example, coaches felt that more time should be spent on 'people skills' and they were highly critical of courses in which they were required to practise on their peers because this further distanced the experience from real-life contexts.

The main finding to note is that the research base concerning football CPD is very small, and the studies are disparate in design, questions asked, methods, sample size and analysis. This makes it difficult to draw strong conclusions. That said, the findings of research that does exist mirror those from research conducted in other professional domains where it is commonly reported that traditional approaches to CPD lack relevance and context-specific knowledge. Importantly, the evidence is clear: when CPD is deemed irrelevant for coaches' individual needs, they simply ignore the new CPD material and continue with what they know, while giving the impression that they are taking new ideas on board. In the literature on teaching, there is growing evidence of Day's (1999) contention that CPD will remain ineffective if it fails to take into account the complexity of teachers' lives in practice. The same would appear to apply to coaching.

FA case study research

Research questions

The research reported in this chapter addressed the following questions (with the methods in brackets):

1. What is already known about CPD undertaken by football coaches? (Desk study)
2. How does the model of CPD for football coaches compare to CPD models in other selected professional fields in and beyond sport? (Desk study)

3. What assumptions are made about learning in football coach CPD by key FA policy-makers and is it feasible to reach a consensus view that has links to the literature? (Face-to-face interviews)
4. What implicit and explicit learning theories underpin the current CPD model for football and what are the implications? (Logic model analysis)

The project was conducted over a period of six months (March to August 2012). The aim of the research was to clarify the basis upon which CPD for football coaches is designed and developed, and identify common characteristics of effective CPD practice from football and other relevant research.

Research methods

1. Literature reviews: in the first stage of the project, a systematic review of existing research into CPD for football coaches was undertaken. Second, the extensive literature on CPD in both physiotherapy and teaching CPD were reviewed selectively to identify key themes that are relevant to The FA context.
2. Interviews: semi-structured interviews were undertaken with key FA stakeholders between May and August 2012. Respondents were: a senior executive, three professional club coach educators, three national youth player development coaches, an advisor, two individuals involved in skills development and coaching workforce management, a head of youth coaching and a coaching director.
3. Data analysis: interviews were transcribed verbatim and then analysed independently by two researchers. The final themes represent a synthesis of the two independent analyses. Data selected represent all the data that directly addressed the research questions, and direct quotations illustrate the main points. Finally, a logic model analysis was undertaken to provide a summary of the research findings from across the datasets.
4. Ethical clearance was given by the University of Birmingham Ethics Committee. The respondents signed consent forms, and the researchers have undertaken to anonymise the comments made by individuals.

Research findings

RQ1: what is already known about the CPD undertaken by football coaches?

A summary of the research findings on research question 1 (RQ1) is presented in the introduction so in this section we simply offer some additional information on the state of the field. It is important to remember that the literature on CPD for football coaches is sparse; indeed, the main finding of the systematic review of literature in this area was that there was very little to find! Moreover, what was retrieved is difficult to compare because the studies were so different in design, questions asked, methods, sample size and analysis. An example of the search process can be seen in Table 3.1; as it illustrates, when using these search terms a total of five papers met the inclusion criteria. It is also worth remembering that these databases are global so, for example, a search using the term 'football' resulted in numerous articles about American football. Here again, however, there were few studies on CPD.

Table 3.1 illustrates the search protocols and terms used in the review of literature, along with the returns from each database. In the final cut, a total of five separate articles were found and retrieved that met the inclusion criteria. Of those papers that were deemed relevant to the review but irretrievable, a further three were accessed via the use of Google Scholar.

As noted earlier, it was difficult to draw meaningful conclusions from this first stage of the research, but it is interesting to note that the findings of these five studies align closely with the evidence to be found in the much larger research base on CPD in physiotherapy and an even larger base in teaching. We can, therefore, add to the evidence base on CPD for football coaches by learning lessons from the studies in other professional fields. Two fields were selected that, for different reasons, have some connections with coaching: physiotherapy and teaching.

TABLE 3.1 Search protocols and terms used in the review of literature along with the returns from each database

	ERIC		Zetoc		Web of Science		Sports Discus	
	Returns	*Relevant, abstract read and available*	*Returns*	*Relevant, abstract read and available*	*Returns*	*Relevant, abstract read and available*	*Returns*	*Relevant, abstract read and available*
Coach learning AND soccer	15	1	8	1	39	2	20	1
Coach education AND soccer	55	0	11	2	61	4	57	1
Coach development AND soccer	26	0	10	0	68	1	60	2
Professional development AND soccer	6	0	28	0	97	0	52	1
CPD AND soccer	0	0	0	0	0	0	0	0

RQ2: how does the model of CPD for football coaches compare to CPD models in other selected professional fields in and beyond sport?

Physiotherapy is a recognised, degree-level profession with clear entry standards and career-trajectories. This means that it is significantly different to coaching, which is still evolving as a profession, although there are groups within football coaching that could reasonably claim to be professionals. It is interesting to note that despite this important difference, many of the critiques of CPD are the same as those found in the football coaching literature. In this review, a total of 20 articles were found and retrieved (this number excludes duplicated papers found in different databases). In addition to this, the websites of physiotherapy's registering bodies within the UK and Ireland were also used as sources of information.

More research has been conducted on CPD in physiotherapy because it is an established profession. The clinical nature of the setting (largely based on the imperative for patient care) requires mandatory CPD hours/credits with clearly set tariffs and, in echoes of some football CPD, a direct link to the retention of a licence to practice. Despite the differences, overall the research echoes findings on CPD from other fields, including the prevalence of informal learning, lack of time and management support for professional learning and an inadequate CPD evaluation process that tends to evaluate attendance rather than learning. Interestingly, web-based and computer-assisted learning (CAL) are becoming increasingly popular, particularly across the medical industry. In addition, both journal clubs and professional portfolios are common features of CPD, although the latter are often deemed to be ineffective in supporting learning. As is the trend within the wider CPD literature, it is difficult to find robust evidence that links different forms of CPD to impact on specific parts of practice (Dowds & French, 2008; O'Sullivan, 2004). French and Dowds' (2008) review of CPD literature contends that what little research exists within physiotherapy is restricted to formal activities, when in fact the majority of CPD undertaken is informal.

The research base on CPD in teaching is very extensive, so in this project the aim was to provide an overview of the findings that are relevant for football CPD. Interestingly, despite being an education profession whose business is learning, this profession seems to have had little success in establishing an effective CPD structure (although recent developments in professional learning communities are promising) (Lieberman & Miller, 2008). There has been a lot of research in the teaching field, including large experimental measures, of the impact of teacher CPD on learning outcomes. The findings suggest that it is very difficult to make direct links between any single CPD activity and specific pupil learning outcomes, although it is also noted that evaluation measures have often been poor (Guskey & Yoon, 2009). It certainly seems clear that no one form of CPD can meet the learning needs of all teachers all of the time.

The nature, quality and effectiveness of teachers' career-long professional learning have been reported as a concern, both nationally and internationally (Wayne et al., 2008). In Europe, contemporary national policies on education, teacher education and CPD are underpinned by visions of a 'knowledge-driven' society in which lifelong learning is a key feature. The vision is that with adequate and sustained support, citizens/employees should develop their capacities to become autonomous and independent learners who are able to be innovative, think critically and creatively, work collaboratively and take risks (August *et al.*, 2006; European Commission, 2008). It is interesting to note that these capacities are also those identified by The FA as being important for both coaches and players (see also the data from interviews with stakeholders below).

The findings of research on a professional group that could be deemed closest to football coaches – physical education (PE) teachers – also mirror the wider CPD research. Just like their colleagues in other areas of the school curriculum, PE teachers have long argued that professional development fails to meet their needs. For example, research by Armour and Yelling (2004a, 2004b, 2007) found that PE teachers' CPD experiences were lacking coherence, relevance, challenge and progression. In addition, PE teachers held strong beliefs about the value of learning collaboratively with and from professional colleagues, but were also aware that this form of informal, collaborative learning wasn't viewed as 'real' CPD by their schools. On the other hand, when they attended an official CPD 'course' which required them to abandon their pupils for a day and which could be, ultimately, ineffective, they were often able to count this as CPD by recording evidence of attendance as sufficient evidence of learning (Armour & Yelling, 2007). In other words, the attendance model of learning prevails in this profession too.

The results of these literature searches contain strong messages about the nature of ineffective CPD and point to clear areas of agreement across professional boundaries. In the next stage of the research, therefore, we asked key stakeholders about their aspirations for CPD in The FA.

RQ3: what assumptions are made about learning in football coach CPD by key FA policy-makers and is it feasible to reach a consensus view?

It is interesting to note that all interview respondents had a clear vision of the kinds of players they thought should be developed (innovative, creative, technically skilful, thinkers, etc.) and the important characteristics of coaches (motivated, curious, problem solvers and risk takers). There was clear consensus on these points. Similarly, there was a shared belief that CPD should engage coaches in dialogue, be needs-led, allow coaches to make errors, promote creativity and innovation, and be both personalised and sustained. Taken together, these beliefs about coaches, players and CPD seemed to be coherent. It was less clear, however, how these beliefs were reflected in current CPD policy and practice. Furthermore, what was missing was a clear understanding of how the prevailing model of coach CPD could lead to the development of coach learners with the desirable characteristics that were identified; i.e. coaches who are curious, self-motivated, creative, problem-solving and risk taking. Indeed, it can be argued that some of the structures of football and football CPD work against any aspirations to develop these kinds of learners (coaches and players). Yet, unless coaches have opportunities to develop new ways of learning through CPD, it is difficult to see how they can develop players in appropriate ways.

Extracts from the interviews with key stakeholders illustrate the range of views around these points:

> If you understand the purpose of the CPD you'll probably target the CPD better, and derive more benefit from your CPD; if you go along thinking 'oh, I've got to go to this CPD event', then you're a loser before you go so we do start with that.

> Decision-making, encouraging flair, creativity, is at the very top of the list and you can't encourage that and encourage, and do decision making if you're so intense you've got to win, because you're going to be shouting, you're going to be hollering.

> I think one of the criticisms of what we've done in the past is that it's been almost a one-size-fits-all product, so when I say the appropriateness of CPD it's what are my real needs as opposed to the same.

> It's interesting how we haven't often in the past designed our professional education for coaches, or teachers come to think of it, which is even more unforgivable when you think about it, based on anything we know about learning, so it's just very odd.

> I think one of the things for me when people say, 'oh we need coaches that think out of the box', I don't think we've agreed what's in the box.

RQ4: what implicit and explicit learning theories underpin the current CPD model for football?

The logic model shown in Table 3.2 illustrates the claims made in the interview data about the nature and purpose of CPD for football coaches and its link to major anticipated outcomes. What the model illustrates is the aspirations underpinning CPD for football coaches, and it has interesting implications for underpinning learning theories and pedagogies.

Logic models, by their very name, imply a comforting degree of rationality and certainty, yet they are better understood as a relatively simple visual tool for presenting complex ideas and identifying programme gaps and tensions. The model can be read across from the underpinning assumptions, through the inputs that inform actions, and the outputs and outcomes that are the consequences of the actions. It is apparent from this logic model, for example, that between the

TABLE 3.2 Aspirational FA CPD logic model

Underpinning Assumptions	Your planned work – what you intend to do		Your intended results – what you expect to happen		
	RESOURCES/ INPUT i.e. positive or negative factors influencing ability to do your work	ACTIVITIES i.e. what is done with the resources	OUTPUTS i.e. the direct product of activities	OUTCOMES i.e. changes in participants due to the programme	IMPACT i.e. changes in organisations, communities or systems due to the programme
The FA has a role in supporting clubs and youth development. The 'game' in England needs to change to reflect changes elsewhere and to develop a stronger national team.	FA Support	Offer a wide range of age- and position-specific short courses	More coaches taking more CPD qualifications	Coaches who are self-motivated, curious learners and who have the confidence to try new ideas	The development of a large pool of creative, skilful players to feed the club and national game
Clubs buy players from abroad rather than investing in young home players and this needs to change. The game needs players who are technically strong but also creative and innovative. The traditional pipeline of young people into football has been disrupted (more sports options for contemporary youth and more technological distractions).		Expansion of CPD programme delivered to professional coaches *in situ*	Raise the profile of coach education	Coaches develop both their technical and pedagogical skills over time	A youth-friendly model of football coaching that is widely respected in communities with parents supporting the new approach
Youth coaches need to have the pedagogical skills to work effectively with contemporary youth to keep them in the game and to develop the kinds of players sought by the national game.		Online provision Advertise/communicate FA learning	Modelling and leading activity to promote high-quality coaching	The role of The FA in coach education is established	The learning and developmental needs of young people placed at the heart of football coaching
Youth coaches require the same characteristics as those they are trying to develop in players.		Train and support licensed tutors for CPD courses	Increased numbers in a qualified tutor workforce	More young people choose to stay in the game of football resulting in a better image for the game and a larger pool of talent for the club and national game	An improved connection between clubs and The FA in the shared goal of producing unique home-grown players for both clubs and the national game

underpinning assumptions on the left of the model, and the intended impact on the right, there is a need for a different model of coach CPD that could better support coaches to do what is required of them. Currently, there is little evidence of this in practice except, perhaps, in the PCCE/FAYCE programmes that have been piloted and extended. Even these programmes, however, are likely to face ongoing problems in addressing the entrenched structural clash between club and FA/national game goals.

Taking the evidence from the literature review and the interviews together, the logic model illustrates that the key weaknesses in The FA CPD processes are in two areas: pedagogy and consistency of coach learning theory. Regarding pedagogy, it is clear that The FA and its coaches will need to find ways to work more effectively with contemporary youth and, moreover, that parents and clubs need to be educated about the long-term value of a pedagogically sound approach. This will safeguard the flow of young people into football. It is also clear that young people should be encouraged to sample numerous sports, and that far from detracting from football interest and enjoyment, it is likely to enhance both. Second, regarding coach learning theory, it would be helpful for The FA to design CPD processes and structures based on the learning theories that best reflect the kinds of coaches and players they are seeking to develop.

In a recent study on teacher professional learning (Armour & Makopoulou, 2012) it was concluded that one of the main flaws in a CPD system that was being evaluated was a fractured understanding of teachers as learners. As Armour (2011), among others, has argued, teachers could benefit from considering themselves as, primarily, learners rather than as teachers. What this suggests, therefore, is that if coaches could be conceptualised (primarily) as lifelong learners themselves, rather than 'deliverers' of learning to others, they would be more likely to be able to develop the kinds of learning skills that are required to develop new kinds of players. *However, in order for this to happen, traditional conceptualisations of learning need to be challenged.* This step is an essential one because traditional understandings of learning, derived from personal coaching experiences, may conjure up notions of wholly didactic coaching approaches. These approaches on their own are, of course, the very opposite to those required to develop creative and innovative players.

Summary and critical questions

Although there is relatively little research in the specific field of CPD for football coaches, there is evidence that existing provision fails to meet the needs of many coaches. The reasons given include: CPD is divorced from the reality of practice; it does not take into account individual needs; it is not sustained; and evaluation procedures allow for an attendance model of learning – meaning that little changes in practice. Although these comments are based on a variable data base with relatively few studies, they do appear to echo the findings of the analysis of CPD research in other professional fields.

As noted above, there are strong similarities between the findings of research on the effectiveness of CPD in football coaching and the two fields selected as comparators: physiotherapy and teaching. It is important to remember, however, that football coaching is a distinctive field because it has a very diverse workforce (including volunteers) and fewer in coaching are educated to undergraduate degree level and beyond. Perhaps one of the most important points to make is that football coaching can learn from the errors made in other professional fields, and by developing a new model add something novel to the wider CPD research base. In addition, the value of needs-led CPD was mentioned often, as was the importance of matching CPD learning to the developmental stage of each coach. It was recognised, however, that whereas a shared philosophy is emerging around The FA's *Future Game* document, challenges remain in establishing a robust pedagogy fit for contemporary youth and in challenging the existing entrenched football learning culture. There was also some evidence of confusion in the terminology used in training and CPD.

The findings of this research have significance for governing bodies of sport charged with professional development activities, who might find it helpful to consider:

1. How does *each* course and CPD activity reinforce the messages about the kinds of players and coaches that are desired?
2. How do learning theories underpin the design and process of CPD activities – and in what way does the organisation ensure these are *coherent* across all CPD activities?
3. How is CPD *evaluated* to ensure that evaluation processes reinforce – rather than undermine – what is the learning philosophy of the organisation?
4. How are *entrenched* traditional views of learning challenged (often derived from school experiences) and youth player development found in clubs?

References

Armour, K.M. (ed.) (2011). *Sport pedagogy: an introduction for teaching and coaching*. London: Pearson.

Armour, K.M. & Makopoulou, K. (2012). Great expectations: teacher learning in a national professional development programme. *Teaching and Teacher Education*, 28 (3), 336–346.

Armour, K.M. & Yelling, M.R. (2004a). Continuing professional development for experienced physical education teachers: towards effective provision. *Sport, Education and Society*, 9 (1), 95–114.

Armour, K.M. & Yelling, M.R. (2004b). Professional development and professional learning: bridging the gap for experienced physical education teachers. *European Physical Education Review*, 10 (1), 71–94.

Armour, K.M. & Yelling, M.R. (2007). Effective professional development for physical education teachers: the role of informal, collaborative learning. *Journal of Teaching in Physical Education*, 26 (2), 177–200.

August, K., Brooks, R. Gilbert, C., Hancock, D., Hargreaves, D., Pearce, N., Roberts, J., Rose, J. & Wise, D. (2006). *2020 Vision: Report of the Teaching and Learning in 2020 Review Group*. London: DfES Publications.

Brunetti, G.J. (1998). Teacher education: a look at its future. *Teacher Education Quarterly*, Fall, 59–64.

Chesterfield, G., Potrac, P. & Jones, R. (2010). 'Studentship' and 'impression management' in an advanced soccer coach education award. *Sport, Education and Society*, 15 (3), 299–314.

Day, C. (1999). *Developing teachers: the challenges of lifelong learning*. London: Falmer Press.

Dowds, J. & French, H. (2008). Undertaking CPD in the workplace in physiotherapy. *Physiotherapy Ireland*, 29, 11–19.

European Commission (2008). *European Qualifications Framework for Lifelong Learning*. Luxembourg: Office for Official Publications of the European Communities.

French, H. & Dowds, J. (2008). An overview of continuing professional development in physiotherapy. *Physiotherapy*, 94 (3), 190–197.

Guskey, T.R. & Yoon, K.S. (2009). What works in professional development. *Phi Delta Kappan*, March, 495–501.

Hammond, J. & Perry, J. (2005). A multi-dimensional assessment of soccer coaching course effectiveness. *Ergonomics*, 48(11–14), 1698–1710.

Jones, R., Armour, K. & Potrac, P. (2003). Constructing expert knowledge: a case study of a top-level professional soccer coach. *Sport, Education and Society*, 8 (2), 213–229.

Lemyre, F., Trudel, P. & Durand-Bush, N. (2007). How youth-sport coaches learn to coach. *The Sport Psychologist*, 21 (2), 191–209.

Lieberman, A. & Miller, L. (2008). *Teachers in professional communities*. New York: Teachers College.

Nash, C. (2002). Soccer coaching in the USA and Scotland. *International Sport Studies*, 24 (2), 33–44.

Nash, C. (2003). Coaching effectiveness and coach education programmes: perceptions of Scottish and US coaches. *International Sports Studies*, 25 (2), 21–31.

Nelson, L.J. & Cushion, C.J. (2006). Reflection in coach education: The case of the national governing body coaching certificate. *Sport Psychologist*, 20 (2), 174.

O'Sullivan, J. (2004). Continuing professional development: is it beneficial? *Physiotherapy*, 90, 174–175.

Wayne, A.J., Suk Yoon, K., Zhu, P., Cronen, S., & Garet, M.S. (2008). Experimenting with teacher professional development: motives and methods. *Educational Researcher*, 37 (8), 469–479.

4

QUALITY ASSURANCE PROCEDURES IN COACH EDUCATION

William Taylor and Ryan Groom

Introduction

This chapter considers the procedure and practices employed by national governing bodies (NGBs) of sport in their efforts to quality assure their coach education schemes and delivery. In doing so we will first attempt to locate the origins of this commitment and suggest that sporting organisations, both NGBs and other agencies, are being increasingly influenced by commercial and business-related concepts and practices (Millar & Rose, 2008). Second, we will consider some of the research and movements within the field of quality assurance (QA), drawing on work from outside of sport. Third, we will draw on some research commissioned by The Football Association (FA) in the UK, the aim of which was to move the process of QA away from being seen as one of checking and monitoring standards towards one that can be viewed as a support mechanism that focuses on coach tutor development. The chapter concludes by offering a number of research questions that, hopefully, will inspire future enquiry, and also prompt NGBs and other interested individuals to think critically as they struggle to develop processes that go beyond a sterile application of QA.

While there has always been a desire for NGBs to support coaching and coach education in the best way possible, these organisations have come under increasing pressure from central government, funding bodies and education agencies to adopt new policies and their accompanying practices (Green & Houlihan, 2005). A combination of limited financial independence, pressing internal priorities and ongoing political pressure to meet sports policy objectives and deadlines has meant that the adoption of prescribed notions of how to manage issues of quality in the field of coach education and delivery has received scant critical consideration (Taylor & Garratt, 2012). In addition, there has been little, if any, internal research undertaken by NGBs into 'how best to make these requirements fit their current practice' (Taylor & Groom, 2014). Any adoption of these practices is not isolated to particular areas of sport policy, but rather is wrapped up in a wider belief that the importing of business and commercial practices *per se* is the best way for sporting NGBs to operate (Andrews & Silk, 2002). So, now sport organisations in the UK must commit to be 'outward facing', treat their coaches and other members of the coaching community as 'customers in their own right', and consider the quality of the services they consume. This movement brings with it new ways to think and speak about coach education; for example, coaching courses are now 'products', those coaches keen to pass on their knowledge to others are now part of a 'workforce' and act as 'mentors'. We have coach education managers, learning contracts, regional coach development officers and continuous professional development (CPD) portfolios. As such, we have assimilated the culture of the marketplace into sport and coach education and accompanying this are the mechanisms of auditing and QA (Bush *et al.*, 2013).

Quality assurance as a concept has its roots firmly in industry, more particularly the engineering sectors, and much of the related research and subsequent accepted practices draw heavily on traditional management studies. In turn, their origins are found in the emerging auditing approaches of both Japanese and American industries of the 1970s and 1980s (Travers, 2007). The central commitment here is that QA practices (checking quality, manufacture by a systematic approach, unifying standards across operations, building in quality at each and every stage of operation) were important concepts in increasing quality of the product, reduction of faulty goods and, in turn, improvements in output and profit. This movement, often conceptualised in the form of total quality management (TQM), was deemed to be successful in the manufacturing fields and was rolled out to impact the approach by which employees were managed (Seddon, 2000). It aligned itself to the belief that such a systematic approach can be applied unproblematically to the service arenas where people and social interaction are central to effective service delivery (Berk & Berk, 1993; Milakovich, 1995). Different forms and iterations of QA are now commonplace in the UK health service, education and other public sector provision (Cooke, 2006; Hood *et al.*, 1999). The notion of measuring quality, however it is defined, now manifests itself in the act of being inspected, the observation of practice and being reviewed, and the importance placed on various modes of internal and external auditing. As already mentioned, these QA practices are relatively new developments within NGBs of sport and their coach education schemes. They include the submitting of new programmes of coach education to outside agencies for verification (bodies such as Sports Coach UK), the internal auditing of coach education training and delivery and the benchmarking of awards and processes against sector-related standards.

A number of issues of importance remain; while the coach education systems of sports NGBs are increasingly subject to the mechanism of audit and QA, we have as yet to assess critically the appropriateness of the standards against which we are measured. In addition, the importing of QA practices from the commercial sector may well remain insensitive to the nuanced nature of sport in the UK, particularly when the applications of systems fail to acknowledge the strong volunteer base that underpins much of what constitutes coach education in the UK (Taylor & Garratt, 2012). Notwithstanding these critical perspectives, it should be acknowledged that the utilisation of QA processes may bring with it a number of benefits; for example, it provides assurance to outside agencies and stakeholders that aspects of delivery meet a certain level of minimal operation. In this context, it may be seen as an application of 'risk management practices' in as much as it attempts to tackle delivery issues at the point of inception and, thus, deals with QA concerns where they might be best addressed and before they become a more protracted and, possibly, complex set of concerns (Travers, 2007). In some contexts the implementation of QA mechanisms can be part of a feedback loop by which recurrent issues are identified and 'wrinkles in the system' can be dealt with. These may come in the form of identifying areas where additional training is offered to coach education tutors and managers, delivery procedures are changed because patterns of failure emerge, or where complete coach education programmes require revision as they are deemed no longer fit for their intended purpose. Quality assurance mechanisms have the ability to provide a direct link between the aspirations of NGBs to assure high standards in coach education in the field with those who deliver it. We contend, however, that too often the reality of such procedures fails to exploit the inherent possibilities that QA holds and the opportunity to directly influence delivery. The opportunity to focus on aspects such as tutor development and the sharing of best practice may be lost due to the narrow concerns of checking standards.

We now turn to some empirical research to help contextualise some of these concerns and to provide insight into the procedures undertaken by The FA in efforts to enhance its own coaching education practices (Taylor & Groom, 2014).

The Football Association and the development of QA procedures

Recent research conducted for The FA (Taylor & Groom, 2014) focused on the review of the structure and appropriateness of their then QA mechanisms. Similar to other NGBs of sport in the UK, The FA employs QA procedure across differing levels and stages of their coach education schemes. Their QA processes include aspects such as checking the quality of the workbooks sent out to course participants, making sure that students are registered and meet the course requirements and engaging in on-site QA visitation to review the quality of provision in the field. It was this last element that was the focus of the recent FA research which utilised three data–collection methods: a literature review which considered the published material in coach education and related fields; a number of interviews with individuals and stakeholders involved in QA within The FA and other fields (45 in total); and a desktop survey of The FA's internal QA paperwork. The following findings are a series of extracts from the full research project and, first, we consider the experiences of other sectors in their efforts to quality assure their services.

The experience and practice of QA from other sectors

The desire to improve and monitor the performance and quality of service delivery is a common feature across industry, commerce, education and, increasingly, the sports sector. The use of visiting inspectors and assessors working within a number of differing QA frameworks is now commonplace. To help gain a picture of practice in related domains, interviews were undertaken with QA officers and representatives from a number of sports, commercial and governmental organisations. These interviews proved to be productive in as much as they allowed a picture to emerge of the recent developments within QA from which a number of key themes emerged.

The most noticeable feature, for some bodies, was a shift in the nature of the QA visitation itself; this was particularly prevalent in organisations such as the Environmental Health and the Health and Safety Inspectorates. It was apparent that there had been a change in emphasis, moving from a notion of 'quality assurance' towards one of 'quality enhancement'. The significant shift is that the role of the inspector is now evolving towards one of knowledge exchange and the sharing of good practices and away from inspection against a set of pre-designated criteria. A number of organisations referred to the importance of building a 'relationship culture' and it was suggested by some that this included the creation of an atmosphere whereby visits were welcomed and that this was seen as a positive cultural change.

A QA officer working in the health service dealing with on-site nurse training commented on the introduction of pre-visit paperwork and the resulting change in the agenda of the visit:

> We have worked hard to shift the nature of the visit and what we are about. The new focus is about developing practitioners, not trying to catch them out. We introduced pre-inspection paperwork a number of years ago; it is the responsibility of the training team [those being visited] to check they are compliant with the regulation and sign off as such ... this now allows us to have professional conversations and to give time to advise and support where we can. It is really about quality enhancement and no longer about checking their systems.

It was reported that where the pre-visitation paperwork had been most beneficial was where action points taken from a previous visit had been used as the starting point for the next visit. This linkage between the last and the current visit builds on the concept that each visit is not a one-off event that one 'passes' or 'fails', but rather an ongoing development of the practitioner.

A coach development officer working outside of football gave an example from within sport:

> We try, as much as resources will allow, to make the inspection not 'a one-off event' but just a part of a series of contacts. When we saw them once

every 18 months it was difficult to build a constructive relationship; now with phone calls, Skype meetings and an open-door policy, the quality assurance team are slowly getting more requests for help. I am convinced it is a move in the right direction. Before it was about box ticking; now the inspectors act as a critical friend and develop coach tutors on site.

This development of an atmosphere that opens up the relationships between the QA personnel and those visited into one where it becomes an opportunity for, and development of, enhancement would seem to require additional resourcing, structure and support. Indeed, those organisations that have successfully moved towards a quality enhancement model have identified the need to up-skill the QA workforce. If the individuals involved are to take on mentorship and developmental roles, then this in turn demands more from those charged with these new tasks. Some of the organisations talked to linked the visits to the identification of CPD opportunities. It was felt that CPD-related discussions would be more welcomed if framed within an atmosphere of continual improvement and one directly related to workplace learning. An officer from the Health Inspectorate Wales expressed such views:

> because we are inspecting people practising in their own work place, the appropriateness of CPD training is strengthened. It is pleasing to see that if identified by both parties the additional training seems to be more welcome and hopefully impactful – it has been a slow process getting all to change the way we think but we have slowly got there.

Among those interviewed, those who seemed to have assessed critically the role of QA had incorporated three different elements: first, the creation of a visitation atmosphere which encouraged learning and development; second, pre-visitation paperwork allowed those involved to spend the contact time more productively; and lastly, the visit was an opportunity to identify CPD needs and opportunities.

Experience of FA tutors of the visitation experience

The research undertaken also interviewed a number of groups directly involved in The FA's QA processes. In talking to FA coach education tutors who had experienced a QA visitation while delivering an education or assessment course, there was general acceptance and support for the notion of a QA process and a realisation that the visitation could bring a number of benefits to the tutors and the course in general. One coach tutor expressed: 'It is worthwhile having someone drop in, generally over the years they have been a positive experience, and the courses themselves do not allow much time to sit back and reflect, so yes, on the whole I support them.'

There was an additional feeling, however, that more could be made of the visitation and opportunities were missed for individual development. A recently qualified coach tutor went on to say:

> to be perfectly honest, I need the support, and time spent at the end of the session answering my questions is more productive for me than the written feedback. I would like to see more time devoted to helping and supporting; any system is only as good as the people in it, so support them.

Tutors who had been visited, when asked about what they would like to see improve within the QA process, commonly suggested that they would like more time to talk to QA personnel and an opportunity to place the education delivery being witnessed into an appropriate context:

> I think they need two things: first, more time to see a fuller picture of what is happening, so yeah, spending more time watching, listening and talking to us. We [name of delivery centre omitted] run a tight ship here; however, we are also under pressure to get people the ticket, they want the student to be qualified. If the QA officers were aware of the situation in which we run these courses, maybe they could be more helpful.

Others expressed a desire to experience the visit as a more personalised and constructive event. While there was acknowledgement that The FA needed to check whether certain standards were being met, there was also an implicit call to make the engagement a more potent opportunity for supporting tutors on an ongoing basis. Some tutors admitted to feeling a sense of isolation and that there was little to help them improve. While there were opportunities to work outside their immediate region, and others were asked to observe other coach education courses, there was a feeling that a more direct relationship with FA coach education personnel was required. The evolution of the QA officers' role would facilitate that development.

An additional theme that emerged from the interview data revealed a concern that any visit did affect the nature of the coach education course itself. One tutor suggested that he 'over coached while being watched' and that he felt he 'needed to display competences for the benefit of the QA officers, not necessarily for the guidance of the student'. It was felt that this unnatural reaction to being observed needed to be taken into account and could be mediated by a more relaxed, informal atmosphere.

Consideration of The FA QA officers

Individuals who already had a QA responsibility supported the idea that the remit of the QA officer could be expanded to take on more of a coach education role. There was, however, a realisation that this would likely involve additional training and be more demanding of the individuals involved. Some of those interviewed were concerned that the additional demands placed on QA officers were likely to mean that a number would choose not to take these on and might withdraw from the system, and thus experienced personnel would be lost. One QA officer who had been in the role for 15 years went on to suggest: 'You need to be careful here, if you are asking more of the individuals involved make sure you do not lose those with considerable field-based experience, you will need them to drive through any change.'

It was suggested by one QA officer that they saw many examples of inventive delivery and novel teaching; however, there was, at present, neither time during a visit nor a central mechanism for sharing these elements. They went on to say:

> certainly, the idea of picking up examples of best practice is something that we do not do in a systematic manner at present … apart from feeding back at the regional level meetings or talking to colleagues, I am not sure it goes much further … having a system that captures this and allows it to be cascaded back down to other coach tutors is a great idea.

There was acknowledgement that these changes in approach would require more time spent in the field beyond the present half-day allocation. If the intention was to develop the remit of these visits to involve developmental aspects such as CPD and the transfer of best practice, then the feeling was that a whole day was required to complete the tasks. With this additional time being available, there was a feeling that a more representative picture would be gleaned: 'If we had a whole day that would be ideal, it would allow you to see more of the course and help build an understanding of the development of the delivery over the complete day.'

The research undertaken by The FA, and summarised within this chapter, is one of the few examples whereby sport NGBs have attempted to engage with empirical research on and about their QA procedures. In meeting the resulting recommendations emerging from the research, a commitment to additional resources would be required. These would include a need for further training of QA personnel, as well as the additional cost relating to an increase in the time allocated for each visit. One could argue that, more importantly, there needs to be a commitment to change the focus of the QA process to one that considers that coach education quality is best met by investing in those individuals who deliver the courses and impact directly on the experiences of the learners.

Implications for coach education and the roles and responsibilities of those involved

Any move away from a sterile representation of QA towards one that sees it as an opportunity to enhance the value of coach tutors will require both a cultural shift and an investment in those taking on these new responsibilities. If we assume that there is a positive relationship between investment in any coach education QA system, the quality of those individuals delivering the coach education courses and the standard of coaches they work with, then it seems appropriate that the QA systems are afforded an importance and centrality that in the past they have been denied. This assumption is contingent on a number of principles: first, that if resources are targeted at supporting coach educators in the field and there is investment in their development, then the quality of coach education will be improved; second, with improvements in coach education delivery, appeals and complaints generated from those unhappy with their experiences as students will reduce. This, in turn, will lessen the amount of time administrators of coach education systems will have to devote to dealing with issues of quality generated by complainees. Lastly, if time and attention is given towards raising the quality of those providing coach education, then those involved in working on courses and schemes will feel more valued and are likely to engage with a greater degree of commitment.

This cultural shift towards 'quality enhancement' and away from 'quality assurance' will require a commitment to realign the role QA personnel have to one which is focused on coach tutor development. This, in turn, may require these individuals to undertake additional training and possess a wider array of pedagogical skills. In efforts to be supportive to the coach tutor workforce, this new brand of QA officers will have to adopt a personalised mentoring role and, thus, be more responsive to individual needs. Through this process there will be a need to focus on building relationships that maintain a balance between meeting the wider needs of the NGBs and, at the same time, provide bespoke support for those coach tutors working in the field.

Historically, NGBs have dealt with the problems relating to the increasing demands placed on coach education schemes by qualifying or appointing more personnel. The uncritical assumption is that additional resources in terms of people is the best solution and is, ultimately, what is required. The mantra of more coaches, whatever their role, resulting in more coaching is commonplace; this notion, however, fails to identify that it is more coaching, not more coaches, which is often the better option. Resources should be aimed at increasing the investment in those individuals the organisation has, rather than increasing the number of people involved. Those who feel that they have been invested in often engage in delivering more courses more often; their currency of practice increases and the advantages of fewer, better educated, coach tutors becomes a realisation. Other factors to consider are that fewer individuals taking on these new responsibilities are easier to manage, and they are likely to maintain comparable standards across practice because they are 'busier' and will become familiar more quickly with the requirements of these roles. In focusing on fewer and better-supported QA personnel, any shifts in curriculum or aspects of delivery may be more effectively conveyed to coach tutors as fewer individuals are more engaged with those in need of the information. As already mentioned, consideration should be taken that the increased demands and qualities required of these individuals mean that not all existing QA officers engaged in the past may be able, or wish, to make this transition and take on these expanded roles.

In concert with this re-orientation of the QA officer's role, the demands made on coach tutors would also change. The checking and accounting processes related to coach education courses and the manner in which they meet minimum requirements is now passed on to the coach tutor. With the QA visit and procedures focused on helping the enhancement of delivery, questions such as have the course learners been registered on the programme and have the prerequisites been processed, or is the course staffed within current guidance relating to ratios and are the tutors current and appropriate for the level of delivery, are left to the course director. The use of pre-visitation paperwork, where self-declaration of compliance with NGB structures is the responsibility of those involved in delivery, changes the relationship and atmosphere of any QA visitation. Those delivering individual NGBs' coach provision and engaging with the learners attending such courses are now responsible for their own professional practice and standards of delivery. The NGB QA officer's role is no longer solely to make assurances about whether standards are being met, but rather has shifted to one of supporting those who are undertaking the role in relation to these standards. Those assurances are now the responsibility of those delivering, and in doing so QA moves away from a process that is seen as one that is 'done to you' to one that is 'done with you', building on the coach tutor's own practice and becoming part of the commitment to betterment and a more personal relationship to improving standards.

We suggest that any move to the reorientation of existing and traditional models of QA will take a number of years to embed fully. This realignment will require a skilled and resourceful workforce to take on the transformation from 'quality assurance to quality enhancement' and an ongoing commitment to resourcing from the organisation itself. The repositioning of QA responsibilities and the shift towards remoulding the roles required of QA personnel could bring forth considerable benefits, resulting in improvements in the quality of coach education delivery and, ultimately, better educated coaches practising in the field.

Critical questions and an agenda for future research

The published research into QA within sports coach education is limited in scope and depth and is theoretically immature. This is somewhat surprising considering the increasing attention directed to other aspects of coach education. In efforts to promote further investigation, we offer a number of research questions and prompts with the hope that some of these will generate field-based enquiry and critical discussion among those who wish to see progress in the field of coach education and quality enhancement.

1. In the move from quality assurance to quality enhancement, what additional training requirements would be needed to equip QA coach development officers to fulfil their new roles?

2. Are there limits to what can reasonably be expected in the advancement of quality enhancement while most UK NGB coaching education tutors are volunteer or part-time NGB employees?
3. How might NGBs in sport set their own research agenda with regards to coach education quality enhancement and are there certain elements of the process that require their immediate attention?
4. What are the inherent tensions evident in quality enhancement in coach education between the appropriateness of the central support system and the quality of the coach tutors involved?
5. If quality in coach education has a direct relationship to the standard of coaches it produces and the experiences of those they go on to coach, why has quality assurance, up to this point, been such a neglected research area?

It should be stated that the questions outlined should not be taken as representing all that we still need to know about QA in coach education, nor that all these questions are valid in relation to all sport NGBs QA systems. Indeed, as the sport coaching sector matures, gains confidence and becomes secure enough to generate its own nuanced understanding concerning which systems and processes best suit its needs, it may be the case that the ability to find the right solutions will have its roots in the very coaching practice it seeks to enhance.

References

Andrews, D.L. & Silk, M.L. (eds) (2002). *Sport and neoliberalism: politics, consumption and culture*. Philadelphia, PA: Temple Press.

Berk, J. & Berk, S. (1993). *Total quality management: implementing continuous improvement*. New York: Sterling.

Bush, A.J., Silk, M., Andrews, D. & Lauder, H. (2013). *Sports coaching research: context, consequences and consciousness*. London: Routledge.

Cooke, H. (2006). Seagull management and the control of nursing work. *Employment and Society*, 20 (2), 223–243.

Green, M. & Houlihan, B. (2005). *Elite sport development: policy learning and political priorities*. London: Routledge.

Hood, C., Scott, C., Oliver, J., Jones, G. & Travers, T. (1999). *Regulation inside government: waste-watchers, quality police and sleaze-busters*. Oxford: Oxford University Press.

Milakovich, M. (1995). *Improving service quality: achieving high performance in the public and private sectors*. Delray Beach: St Lucie Press.

Miller, P. & Rose, N. (2008). *Governing the present*. Cambridge: Polity Press.

Seddon, J. (2000). *The case against ISO9000*. Dublin: Oak Tree Press.

Taylor, W.G. & Garratt, D. (2012). Coaching and Professionalisation. In P. Potrac, W. Gilbert & J. Dennison (eds), *The Routledge handbook of sports coaching* (pp. 27–39). London: Routledge.

Taylor, W.G. & Groom, R. (2014). *Review of coaching scheme quality assurance procedures. Report for The Football Association and FA Learning*. Burton: England.

Travers, M. (2007). *The new bureaucracy: quality assurance and its critics*. Bristol: Policy Press.

PART II
Development and support

5

TASK ANALYSIS OF COACH DEVELOPERS

Applications to The FA Youth Coach Educator role

Andrew Abraham

Introduction

In creating the role of The FA Youth Coach Educator (FAYCE) in 2011 The Football Association (The FA) were getting well ahead of the game when it came to coach education. The role was created to work in partnership with youth academies of professional football clubs to support the professional development and practice of youth team coaches. This support, delivered through formal FA courses and one-to-one coach support during coaching sessions, progressed coach education from a remote, decontextualised process to an embedded, meaningful one. In short, the role deliberately blurred the lines between crucial formal coach education and often preferred an informal approach to self-development (Abraham *et al.*, 2010; Mallett *et al.*, 2009; Nelson *et al.*, 2006) of previous approaches. The success of the FAYCE role is dependent on an interaction of key factors; a high-quality formal and informal educational programme and a coach educator capable of delivering it. While The FA were comfortable that they had been able to employ the latter to deliver the former, there was a recognition of a need to be seen to be practising what they were preaching. That is, while the FAYCEs were delivering thought-through programmes of professional development for coaches, there is relatively little known about what makes a coach educator effective. Indeed, there is a paucity of research examining the work of coach developers with only relatively weak descriptions within papers examining the experience of coaches in coach education courses (e.g. Piggott, 2012; Reid & Harvey, 2014). Furthermore, there is also little known as to what the professional development needs of a coach educator (i.e. FAYCE) are. As such this formed the basis for the project reported here. The aims of this project therefore were:

- to examine the role of a coach educator in the field;

- to develop an informed view on the knowledge and skills required to perform the role of a coach educator;
- to identify the detailed requirements and methods of professional development for those engaged as a coach educator (FAYCE).

Theoretical framework: professional judgement and decision-making

In keeping with recent research examining professional practice, I applied the theory of Professional Judgement and Decision-Making (PJDM) and the aligned methodology in this project (e.g. Abraham & Collins, 2011; Kahneman & Klein, 2009; Lipshitz *et al.*, 2001; Vickers *et al.*, 2004). PJDM highlights the connection between practice and decision-making, where the behaviour of practitioners is underpinned by a judgement and decision-making process. For example, coach educators have to be able to improve the coaching knowledge and behaviour of coaches through giving them tasks and teaching them. PJDM is interested in discovering the knowledge and judgements that lead to the decisions that coach educators take to achieve this sort of goal.

Broadly speaking, this research displays that professionals, when practising, engage in two types of decision-making. The first, *intuitive* or *naturalistic decision-making* (NDM), occurs when time is limited and judgements have to be made that are rapid in nature. Alternatively, when greater time is available professionals engage in making judgements that are slower, made with greater thought and deliberation and take a 'classical' approach to problem solving, i.e. *thoughtful* or *classical decision-making* (CDM). In essence, this process broadly reflects the simplistic *plan–do–review* view of practice, where CDM occurs during planning and reviewing, whereas NDM occurs during doing.

However, important distinctions need to be made that define the professional from the lay person. These distinctions relate to the knowledge and skills that professionals have. Professionals have both theoretical and experiential expertise stored in the form of knowledge that is deep, broad and interconnected. Due to extensive critical experience professionals are able to perceive (i.e. from visual and auditory information) patterns in information that allows them to see shortcuts through to understanding problems and/or creating solutions to problems (Abraham & Collins, 2011; Schempp *et al.*, 2006). This skill has been defined as professionals being able to gain a quick *situational awareness* (Klein *et al.*, 2006).

Further to this knowledge, professionals develop their capacity to become more strategic, political and future focused in their planning. As such, professionals develop the capacity to engage in a process termed *nested decision making*:

> where decisions taken at a micro level are embedded (nested) within medium term agendas which themselves are linked to (nested within) longer term aims. As such, naturalistic decisions are explicitly linked to decisions taken at a more classical level when time is available to think through ideas.
>
> *(Abraham & Collins, 2011, p. 380)*

Subsequently, professional practice is underpinned by being able to ground judgements in extensive theoretical, personal and practical expertise. Crucially this is true for both naturalistic and classical judgements. In essence, professional judgement that is made in a classical manner must be a result of much critical, often peer-reviewed[1]/informed thinking and planning emanating from a broad and deep knowledge base. Alternatively, if a professional judgement needs to be made intuitively and in a naturalistic setting, then it must come from extensive practice that allows swift situational analysis, with the ability to pick up key cues in the environment (i.e. facial expressions, subtle changes in body language, subtle changes in performance) that align with ready-made decisions. In both NDM and CDM, professionalism is informed by hours of previous critical thinking and reflection which will more often that not differentiate the lucky or recipe-based practitioner from the intuitive and adaptable professional.

To conclude this brief introduction to PJDM, two final key issues remain. The first is that the capacity to make decisions is initially based on recognising perceptual information that needs to be responded to. In NDM situations this means the capacity to recognise patterns in environmental information that needs to be responded to quickly. For example, recognising facial expressions that suggest a learner is confused, a tone of voice that suggests frustration that may lead to anger. From a CDM perspective, the perceptual skill will be to understand the information that will need to be collected to ensure the problem being addressed is sufficiently understood before it is addressed. The second key issue is that as expertise builds, paradoxically, professionals become much more aware of the uncertainty that exists in everyday practice. Professionals will actively try to address this uncertainty rather than suppress it (Lipshitz & Strauss, 1997). For example, professionals will note that some parts of their practice are not going as planned and, rather than ignoring this or hoping it will just go away, they will reflect on the uncertainty and improve the practice.

Self-regulation and professional development

In addition to having the knowledge and skills required to operate in a professional manner, there are also the skills required to become and remain professional as well. Supplementing the PJDM theory therefore are other cognitive-behavioural and educational ideas that have been shown to be crucial for professional practice. For example, educational research has displayed that professionalism is arrived at through the consistent application of metacognitive skills such as reflecting and thinking about how to think in order to learn more efficiently and effectively (Entwistle & Peterson, 2004). Similarly, performance psychology research has repeatedly displayed that self-regulatory mental skills such as focusing, planning and accurate performance analysis (MacNamara et al., 2010) increase capacity to practice more deliberately. This capacity to deliberately practice is crucial in being able to consistently engage in quality thinking and educational practice and therefore in becoming a high-functioning professional.

This is clearly and deliberately a whistle stop tour of PJDM and metacognitive theory. In summary, therefore, a professional is one who has the knowledge and skills to make judgements and decisions in both naturalistic/intuitive moments and more classical/thoughtful planning and reflective moments. I have outlined this in Table 5.1; the headings in the table also follow through to the results tables, presented later.

TABLE 5.1 Characteristics of expertise

Principle	Characteristic	CDM – thoughtful DM	NDM – intuitive DM
Professional knowledge	Knowledge	Extensive explicit knowledge of what can be done and how it can be done	Extensive repertoire of experience-based ideas and intuitions
	Perceptual skills	Knows what sources of information to search for in order to increase knowledge and awareness	Where to look and listen, when to look and listen, what to look at and listen for, how often
Professional skills	Plan and re-plan nested goals and operations	Develops linked macro, meso and micro goals Creates linked plans for the achievement of the goals	Makes rule-based or intuitive decisions that are aligned with objectives of longer-term plan
	Manage uncertainty	During planning processes uncertainty is embraced, and researched	In limited time uncertainty is dealt with, drawing on repertoire of knowledge and skills
	Organise and engage in professional development and practice	Actively identifies sources of and critically engages in learning and assessment opportunities Deliberately engages in opportunity to read Seeks out and engages with a critical peer group to guide informal learning	Draws knowledge and skills to reflect in practice
	Evaluate performance and work on weaknesses	Draws on relevant sources of data and benchmarks of expert practice to honestly and critically analyse and reflect on self and create self-development goals on an ongoing basis	
	Cope with job and self-improvement pressures	Employs metacognitive strategies to maintain focus and work to priorities when under pressure	
	Stay aware of what others in similar positions are doing	Keeps abreast of innovations and improvements in practice being made elsewhere and tries to find ways of outperforming peers	

Source: adapted from Klein & Militello (2005), and informed by Entwistle & Peterson (2004) and MacNamara et al. (2010).

Method

Applied cognitive task analysis as a method for investigating PJDM

Collectively, given the professional practice nature of the FAYCE role, the broad theories of PJDM, self-regulation and mental skills bring a useful lens through which to examine the role. Indeed, decision-making as a basis for understanding practice has been used in several domains such as nursing, combat, psychology, coaching and firefighting (Abraham & Collins, 2011; Kahneman & Klein, 2009; Martindale & Collins, 2007; Salas *et al.*, 2008). Within these domains the method of *Applied Cognitive Task Analysis* (ACTA) has often been deployed to capture the decision-making practice of professionals; as such this was the process followed in this study. ACTA has four stages (Gore & McAndrew, 2009).

Stage 1: creation of a task diagram

A task diagram is developed to try to summarise the core tasks and decisions that define a professional role. In order to meet this demand I drew on the model of coach development decision-making (Figure 5.1) developed by Abraham *et al.* (2009).

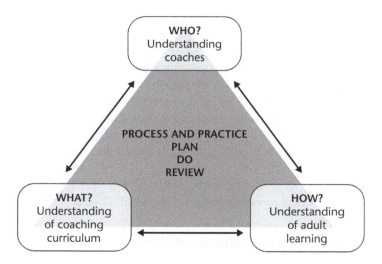

FIGURE 5.1 The coach development decision making model (adapted from Abraham *et al.*, 2009).

Note: the arrows represent the need to consider interaction between areas as defined by task 5, process and practice.

This model was developed based on a review of available evidence and literature and summarised six broad tasks. These six tasks are summarised as:

1. Understand context, strategy and politics: understanding the culture of the situation that is being worked in and adapting behaviour.
2. Who – understand the coach: understanding the coach(es)'s motivations, needs and wants.
3. How – understand adult learning and development: understanding how to most effectively develop learning environments to support adult learning.
4. What – understand coaching curriculum development: understanding the curriculum that will need to be delivered to support coaches in their development.
5. Process and practice: understanding the process and practice of coach development.

The final task reflects that tasks 1–5 are completed by a person. As such a person's capacity to understand their impact on the coach education and development process (i.e. their ability to self-regulate) also represents a task to be completed:

6. Task – understand self: understanding own goals, strengths and limitations, striving to improve when the opportunity exists.

Participants and process

Drawing on this task diagram and the theoretical principles of PJDM, three[2] sets of related data from three different sets of participants were collected in this study. Participant group 1 were eight (seven male, one female) sport federation coach education managers drawn from a range of team and individual sports.

The second group were three (all male) coach developers engaged in formal mentoring roles in one-to-one development programmes with coaches from various sports.

The third group were five (four male, one female) coach educators engaged in delivering workshops as part of overall programmes of coach development.

Stage 2: knowledge audit through interview

Group 1 were engaged in an interview lasting 60–90 minutes. The focus of the interview was to establish the knowledge and skills required to engage in being a professional educator using the six tasks defined in Figure 5.1.

Stage 3: observation and debrief in practice

Both group 2 and 3 were observed in practice and field notes were made. The focus of the field notes was again focused around how the participant was engaging in the six tasks. Three members of group 2 and two members of group 3 were engaged in post-session discussions to draw out reasoning for their behaviour where possible.

Stage 4: results – creation of cognitive demands table

In keeping with the suggestions of Gore and McAndrew (2009), the analysed data were written up as six cognitive demands (that is, these are the demands met by coach developers drawing on knowledge and skills in order to make classical or naturalistic decisions) using the six tasks identified in stage 1. The tables were constructed around the four main concepts presented in Table 5.1:

1. Professional skills
2. Professional knowledge
3. CDM
4. NDM.

Due to issues of space, edited versions of the full tables are shown here. More detailed tables can be found in the associated conference paper (Abraham *et al.*, 2013).

TABLE 5.2 Task 1: understanding the context

	CDM – *thoughtful DM*	NDM – *intuitive DM*
Professional skills	Actively engages in working with relevant FA policy when implementing role Conducts an informed analysis of organisational, group and individual strategy, politics and behaviour	Has a strong situational awareness of goings on in working environment Proactively and reactively recognises and responds to opportunities to support and progress stakeholders towards achievement of nested goal
Professional knowledge	Works to an integrated mental model that encompasses a broad and deep knowledge base around relevant policy, strategic, emotional and political intelligence	Has recourse to a rich set of critiqued experiences of working within complex relationship situations

TABLE 5.3 Task 2: understanding the coach

	CDM – thoughtful DM	NDM – intuitive DM
Professional skills	Works with the coach to review current capabilities, set personalised goals and monitor, review and regulate progress towards set goals Builds and maintains effective relationships with the coach	Has strong situational awareness of coaches' working environment and its demands Proactively and reactively recognises and responds appropriately to moments of coach worry and/or stress when working with the coach
Professional knowledge	Draws on connections between life experiences and contemporary applied theories from social psychology, performance psychology and sociology to critically evaluate, understand and plan for changing coaches' behaviours Draws on rich mental model of what coaching is and how it changes at different levels of competence to facilitate goal setting and coach tracking	Has recourse to a rich set of critiqued experiences of working with coaches where cues in the environment are accurately connected to a limited set of 'correct' solutions

TABLE 5.4 Task 3: understanding adult learning

	CDM – thoughtful DM	NDM – intuitive DM
Professional skills	Develops and monitors relevant learning environments, tasks and communication strategies to meet learning goals Designs, delivers and evaluates meaningful learning opportunities and environments that meet the long-, medium- and short-term learning needs of coaches	Has strong situational awareness of the quality of learning environments Recognises uncertainty in everyday practice and selects relevant coping strategy
Professional knowledge	Works to an integrated mental model that encompasses a broad and deep knowledge base of learning theories and their application to classroom, workshop, online, work-based, community and assessment learning opportunities	Has recourse to a rich set of critiqued experiences within the domains of operation where cues in the environment are accurately connected to a limited set of correct solutions

TABLE 5.5 Task 4: understanding the coaching curriculum

	CDM – *thoughtful DM*	NDM – *intuitive DM*
Professional skills	Designs and/or understands developed coach development curricula that is aligned to FA coach development pathways/FA courses and to the needs of individual coaches Analyses best practice coaching to maintain currency in coaching curriculum	Has strong situational awareness of how well curriculum is being delivered. Also a strong awareness of how well curriculum is being received and worked with by coaches Recognises uncertainty in coaches relating to content to be learned and responds appropriately
Professional knowledge	Works to an integrated mental model that encompasses a broad and deep knowledge base relating to what good coaching is Draws on connections between life experiences and contemporary applied theories from coaching science, developmental psychology and performance psychology to form clear rationale for coach curriculum	Has recourse to a rich set of critiqued experiences within the domains of operation where cues in the environment are accurately connected to a limited set of correct solutions

TABLE 5.6 Task 5: understanding of process and practice

	CDM – *thoughtful DM*	NDM – *intuitive DM*
Professional skills	Makes effective and informed decisions that reflect the big picture of coach development relating to the planning, implementation, monitoring, evaluation and regulation of nested goals and programmes of development Recognises and resolves problematic and atypical issues through the generation of innovative strategies and solutions	Is aware of goings on in working environment Proactively and reactively recognises and responds to opportunities in everyday work to support and progress stakeholders towards achievement of nested goal
Professional knowledge	Works to an integrated and explicit mental model of coach development that encompasses a breadth and depth of knowledge in the domains of: understanding process and practice of coach development, understanding the coach, understanding coaching, understanding adult learning and development, understanding context, strategy and politics, understanding self	Has recourse to a rich set of critiqued experiences within the domains of operation where cues in the environment are accurately connected to a limited set of correct solutions

TABLE 5.7 Task 6: understanding of self

	CDM – thoughtful DM	NDM – intuitive DM
Professional skills	Conducts critically informed, evidence-based self-analysis in order to examine, expose and challenge the congruence of intentions, assumptions and beliefs with practice Works towards professional standards and values	Strives to recognise opportunities for self-development and to work towards personal goals
Professional knowledge	Draws on contemporary concepts and applied theories of coaching expertise, reflection, social psychology, performance psychology and sociology to critically evaluate the reasoning and resources of own behaviour and practice in order to generate development goals and action plans	Has recourse to a rich understanding of self that recognises strengths and weaknesses in knowledge, skills and personal effectiveness Works to a mental model of personal effectiveness, excellence, professional values and ethics

Implications

A cursory glance through the (few) job descriptions that appear for coach developers in job adverts suggests that the results presented in Tables 5.2–5.7 have gone much further towards defining the role of coach developers – a core aim of this project. Typically these job descriptions display a lack of differentiation and definition between professional knowledge and skills. This leads to nebulous statements, often lacking definition, with their focus being around experience, leadership and operational factors. While not surprising or unusual in poorly defined/immature professional vocations, this does limit the capacity to recruit and/or develop emerging and even established professionals in this domain. Deductively analysing the coach developer role through the lens of PJDM and the coach development model has offered a thorough insight into the role of a coach developer. Developing cognitive demands tables (Gore & McAndrew, 2009) has served a relevant and meaningful purpose by offering a (relatively) precise and concise overview of the role, thus progressing research forward. Furthermore, it is against this definition that professional development approaches can be developed.

Further examination of the results in Tables 5.2–5.7 does reveal a level of replication of skills and knowledge. This should not be surprising, however; the tables (and the domains they reflect) are not meant to be orthogonal, they represent parts of one big picture of being a coach developer. Furthermore, creating the tables through multiple sources of data means that they are informed through a wide peer group, thus removing the chance of bias and ideas being missed.

As such, within the under-researched role of coach developers, these tables offer a significant addition to the literature and to coach developers. The tables offer the capacity for a benchmarking exercise against which the role demands of a coach development job can be mapped. Also, the current skills and knowledge of both recently employed and experienced coach developers can be challenged against the content of the tables. Finally, analysing both the role demands and the capacity of coach developers to meet those demands allows informed judgements to be made about professional development needs and programmes to be created.

Caution is needed, however. These tables are created from multiple participants who complete the role of coach developer across different contexts with differing goals. Consequently, the tables are cumulative in nature and therefore not reflective of one single person. In other words, the tables are aspirational. So while they can be useful in the ways described in the previous paragraph, their limitations must also be recognised.

The tables are a well informed (i.e. informed by theory and practice) and succinct summary of the demands of a coach developer role based on the participants involved in the study and a summary of relevant research in the area of PJDM. They are a source of evidence that can inform self-analysis and/or the development of learning outcomes or professional competences for professional development programmes. Indeed, the follow-up work from this project was to develop a bespoke Postgraduate Certificate in Coach Education to serve as a formal professional development qualification for the FAYCE staff. The course created three modules with learning outcomes aligned with the PJDM view of the role and the demands of the six broad task tables. An overview of this approach is shown in Table 5.8 – different shading displays where the emphasis of content maps across; darker shading reflects a greater emphasis.

TABLE 5.8 How module aims and outcomes map to six domains of knowledge and skills

Domain	Modules		
	Understanding expertise	Coach education: an overview	Coach education: personalised learning
1 Task: understanding club and FA context, strategy and politics	██		
2 Task: understanding the coach			██
3 Task: understanding adult learning and development		██	
4 Task: understanding coaching curriculum			
5 Task: process and practice			
6 Task: understand self			

Summary and critical questions

Research examining the work of coach developers is still in its infancy; this project has offered some clear views on what the role entails and therefore what the professional development demands are. However, other sport coach development bodies interested in professional development for their coach developers should think critically (CDM!) about what their own needs are. To conclude, therefore, I offer five critical questions to guide this level of thought:

1. What is the context within which governing bodies are aiming to develop coach developers? Will these people be employed to develop novice/volunteer coaches or professional coaches or somewhere in between? What are the political drivers/strategy behind this?
2. Based on having a view of the type of coach educator required, what are the key tasks that coach educators will have to complete across the six task areas? Also, are there priorities based on the answers to question 1?
3. What are the professional skills and knowledge that the coach educators will require in order to complete these tasks? How does this play out in role/job descriptors?
4. What will be the professional development and/or recruitment needs based on the answers to the first three questions?
5. Consider how the answers to the previous four questions may lay the foundation for professional development and review meetings.

Acknowledgements

This work has been made possible through the funding of Sports Coach UK, UK Sport and The Football Association.

Notes

1 Peer review is commonly viewed as a domain of getting research into journals. However, in this instance it is used more holistically, where a coach's or coach developer's peers would act as the peer review.
2 Due to the scarcity of full-time 'professional' coach educators and in order to get as full a picture as possible it was necessary to draw on data from these three populations.

References

Abraham, A. & Collins, D. (2011). Taking the next step: ways forward for coaching science. *Quest*, 63 (4), 366–384.

Abraham, A., Collins, D., Morgan, G. & Muir, B. (2009). Developing expert coaches requires expert coach development: replacing serendipity with orchestration. In A. Lorenzo, S. J. Ibanez & E. Ortega (eds), *Aportaciones Teoricas Y Practicas Para El Baloncesto Del Futuro*. Sevilla: Wanceulen Editorial Deportiva.

Abraham, A., Muir, B. & Morgan, G. (2010). *UK Centre for Coaching Excellence scoping project report: national and international best practice in Level 4 coach development.* Sports Coach UK.

Abraham, A., Morgan, G., North, J., *et al.* (2013). Task analysis of coach developers: applications to The FA Youth Coach Educator role. In H. Chaudet, L. Pellegrin & N. Bonnardel (eds), *Proceedings of the 11th International Conference on Naturalistic Decision Making (NDM 2013)* (pp. 21–24). Available: www.ndm11.org/proceedings/papers/ndm11-175.pdf, accessed 8 November 2013,

Entwistle, N.J. & Peterson, E.R. (2004). Conceptions of learning and knowledge in higher education: relationships with study behaviour and influences of learning environments. *International Journal of Educational Research*, 41, 407–428.

Gore, J. & McAndrew, C. (2009). Accessing expert cognition. *The Psychologist*, 22 (3), 218–219.

Kahneman, D. & Klein, G.A. (2009). Conditions for intuitive expertise: a failure to disagree. *American Psychologist*, 64 (6), 515–526.

Klein, G. & Militello, L. (2005). The knowledge audit as a method for cognitive task analysis. In H. Montgomery, R. Lipsitz, & B. Brehmer (eds), *How professionals make decisions*. Mahwah, NJ: Lawrence Erlbaum Associates.

Klein, G., Moon, B. & Hoffman, R. (2006). Making sense of sensemaking 1: alternative perspectives. *IEEE Intelligent Systems*, 21 (4), 70–73. Retrieved from http://xstar.ihmc. us:16080/research/projects/EssaysOnHCC/Perspectives on Sensemaking.pdf, accessed 25 February 2014.

Lipshitz, R. & Strauss, O. (1997). Coping with uncertainty: a naturalistic decision-making analysis. *Organizational Behavior and Human Decision Processes*, 69 (2), 149–163.

Lipshitz, R., Klein, G., Orasanu, J. & Salas, E. (2001). Focus article: taking stock of naturalistic decision making. *Journal of Behavioral Decision Making*, 14, 331–352.

MacNamara, Á., Button, A. & Collins, D. (2010). The role of psychological characteristics in facilitating the pathway to elite performance: part I – identifying mental skills and behaviors. *The Sport Psychologist*, 24(1), 52–73.

Mallett, C.J., Trudel, P., Lyle, J. & Rynne, S.B. (2009). Formal vs. informal coach education. *International Journal of Sports Science and Coaching*, 4(3), 325–364.

Martindale, A. & Collins, D. (2007). Enhancing the evaluation of effectiveness with professional judgment and decision making. *The Sport Psychologist,* 21, 458–474.

Nelson, L.J., Cushion, C.J. & Potrac, P. (2006). Formal, nonformal and informal coach learning: a holistic conceptualisation. *International Journal of Sports Science & Coaching*, 1 (3), 247–259.

Piggott, D. (2012). Coaches' experiences of formal coach education: a critical sociological investigation. *Sport, Education and Society*, 17 (4), 535–554.

Reid, P. & Harvey, S. (2014). We're delivering Game Sense … aren't we? *Sports Coaching Review*, 3(1), 80–92.

Salas, E., DiazGranados, D., Klein, C., Burke, C.S., Stagl, K.C., Goodwin, G.F. & Halpin, S.M. (2008). Does team training improve team performance? A meta-analysis. *Human Factors*, 50 (6), 903–933.

Schempp, P.G., McCullick, B.A. & Sannen Mason, I. (2006). The development of expert coaching. In R. Jones (ed.), *The sports coach as educator* (pp. 145–161). Abingdon: Routledge.

Vickers, J.N., Reeves, M.-A., Chambers, K.L. & Martell, S. (2004). Decision training: cognitive strategies for enhancing motor performance. In A.M. Williams & N.J. Hodges (eds), *Skill acquisition in sport: research theory and practice* (pp. 103–120). London: Routledge.

6

THE APPLICATION OF REFLECTIVE PRACTICE

Reflective learning in the education and practices of FA football coaches

Jenny Moon

Introduction

This chapter concerns the rationale for, the development and the conduct of a Football Association (FA) project on reflective practice for coach educators and coaches. Much of the content of the chapter supports the introduction of reflective practice into any sport coaching situation.

'Reflective practice' is a term widely used in education and professional development. The FA has, for a while, encouraged reflection in courses for coach development through various means – for example, through the use of prompts for written reflection in training materials (e.g. boxes to fill with reflective writing) or in reviews of training. However, there has been inconsistency in the use of reflection and variable understanding of it in both theory and practice. Coach educators have not known how to facilitate the learning of such practices and in particular there has been little distinction between superficial description and the deep reflection from which good learning can emerge

These observations led to The FA 'Application of reflective practice (for coaches)' project that provided background thinking on reflective practice and reviewed the potential of reflective learning to support football coaching. Within the project, work was also done on the design for a bespoke training programme on reflective practice for coach educators. In what was regarded as a second part to the project, the course was subsequently conducted.

So why is the practice of reflection (reflective practice) important in coaching and coach education? There are difficulties in researching a constructed term such as reflection (or reflective learning – used here synonymously) and as a result the literature is diverse. Furthermore, the contexts of research vary. For example, reflective learning may be studied within the following situations:

- coaching modules in sport science or other university programmes as support for the programme (e.g. Carson, 2008; Knowles *et al.*, 2001; Demers *et al.*, 2006);
- explicit introduction within a coach education course with or without expectation that coaches will continue to use reflection after the course;
- encouragement of reflection in the field – e.g. reflective discussion between peers regarding issues in play/training, mentoring, etc. (e.g. Carson, 2008; Knowles *et al.*, 2001; Light, 2004; Demers *et al.*, 2006; Harvey *et al.*, 2010; Hughes *et al.*, 2009; Jones & Turner, 2006; Roberts, 2011);
- case study research on reflections of coaches' prior or current experiences in learning to coach (experts and novices) (e.g. Gilbert & Trudel, 2001; Knowles *et al.*, 2006; Nelson & Cushion, 2006; Werthner & Trudel, 2006; Erikson *et al.*, 2007; Nash & Sproule, 2009; Piggott, 2012);
- studies on the theory of reflection in sport coaching (e.g. Cushion *et al.*, 2003; Buysse *et al.*, 2003; Light, 2004; Trudel *et al.*, 2010, 2013; Gilbert & Trudel, 2013; Trudel & Gilbert, 2013; Abraham & Collins, 1998).

Reflection may be introduced explicitly or covertly. For example, peer discussion groups may be reflective (Trudel & Gilbert, 2013), and mentoring should be a reflective process (e.g. Knowles *et al.*, 2006; Nelson & Cushion, 2006, Trudel *et al.*, 2013). In such situations as discussion groups, review or mentoring processes, the word 'reflection' may not be used – and there may be differing consequences for the reflective outcome. Terminology needs to be decided carefully.

It seems that, in the literature, the closer the description is to the implementation of reflective practices, the more sketchy is the coverage in the literature on reflective learning. Writers/researchers may simply equate reflective practice with one of the well-known models of reflection without question and operate within that model (e.g. the Kolb cycle of experiential learning (Kolb, 1984) or practicums (Schon, 1987)). For all these reasons, it is difficult to draw conclusions with regard to the value of or best ways to implement reflective practices. Indeed, for the same reasons it is difficult to make firm statements even about how coaches become more expert in their coaching activities. Some relevant generalisations in that respect are that successful coaches tend to be reflective (Abraham & Collins, 1998; Potrac *et al.*, 2002). They seem to be able to learn effectively from experience – and that requires reflection (Nelson & Cushion, 2006; Werthner & Trudel, 2006; Turner *et al.*, 2012). As part of that process, they have become better at working out ways of using reflection and in particular in managing and reflecting on multiple sources of knowledge (Nelson & Cushion, 2006).

FA case study research: key concepts

Research issues

The research questions for The FA 'Application of reflective practice' project included the following:

- What is a useful definition of reflection for the context of coach education (i.e. consideration of underpinning theories)?
- Why might it be important for coaches to engage effectively (i.e. sufficiently deeply) and what are other benefits (e.g. to The FA, coach educators themselves, players, etc.)?
- What is an effective form of a bespoke training programme for FA coach educators?
- What might be the impact of reflective practice on coaches and coach educators?

The links between theory and practice in terms of reflective practice are discussed by Moon (2004). The outcomes of such considerations were paramount in shaping the content and design of the courses. The main course to be designed was for a selected group of coach educators (termed Course A here), and the second was to be delivered by the Course A attendees to the coaches within their responsibility (Course B). It was intended, therefore, that all FA coaches from grassroots to those in professional situations were to be exposed to Course B. The project was started in late 2013 and the final report was submitted in April 2014. Subsequently, Course A was implemented for a group of coach educators in late 2014. An internal course handbook was prepared as a resource for Course A. The learning outcomes of Course A focused on the development of Course B in which coaches would be participants. They were:

> At the end of Course A, participants will be ready and able to run a one-day course (Course B), which enables coaches on that course to:
> - demonstrate that they can articulate reflective thinking at a reasonable depth;
> - show that they have considered the potential value of a more reflective approach in their coaching for their own practice and that of the players with whom they work;
> - specify some practical ways in which they can introduce reflective learning into their coaching and into the actions of players.

In terms of methodology, discussion of what reflection is was largely based on the researcher's prior research (Moon, 1999a, 1999b, 2004, 2006, 2008), and in particular her experience of running workshops for different professional and educational groups, and within the project, discussions with coaches. A particular concern was making reflective activities palatable to coaches, some of whose background might involve little formal education. The course was three sessions – one full day and two half days. The 'gaps' provided time for participants to practice reflection in set tasks.

This chapter is being written at the stage at which Course A is completed. It was anticipated that Course A participants would now be conducting development work towards the final version and delivery of Course B (to coaches). However, instead of the immediate development of Course B, there is a change of plan. Now a new (three full days) version of Course A (A1) will be delivered to all The FA coach educators who were not participants in Course A (see next section).

Key concepts

This section reviews some key concepts in the work on application of reflective practice.

The first research questions queried the importance of reflective practice. Such thinking needed to underpin the content and design of the courses by providing justification for them. The project identified many situations in which reflection might lead to better decision-making in coaching and the game of football. Examples are reflection on:

- a specific game and its outcomes;
- on a coach's coaching activities and attitudes, his style of interaction, expectations of players, etc.
- on his role within The FA – how he has progressed in learning to be a coach, how he can learn more, how he sees himself in terms of leadership, etc.;
- on more general political and social issues or the place of football in society, etc.

Beyond consideration of what coaches might reflect on, other questions – and corresponding responses – had to be anticipated:

- How do I know what I should reflect on? How do I notice things?
- Where do I reflect? (Possible responses could be in peer discussion, through mentoring situations, in critical friend pairings, etc.)?
- How do I record my reflection? (Voice recording, notebook, photographs, etc.)
- How can I find time to reflect?
- Do I just reflect about my strengths and weaknesses or about other things?
- They say too much introversion is self-indulgent – so why are we doing it?
- I don't do much reading and writing, how can I cope with written stuff?

Turning to reflection itself, there are many models of reflection, so in this project it has been important to clearly lay out the conceptualisation on which the material is based. Reflection is seen here to have the following characteristics (based on Moon, 2004):

- It is a form of thinking but it operates on complex or ill-structured knowledge, not simple ideas.
- People reflect largely on what they know already – though they pull in other ideas where these can deepen their reflection.
- There may be a specific input to reflection (e.g. the coach says: 'Reflect on your moves in play in the last ten minutes'), or people are simply reflective (e.g. musing on the match on the drive home). Both are valuable reflection.

- There may be a specific conclusion drawn from reflection (e.g. 'I can see now that I should not have intervened at that point') or the outcome may be greater knowledge or recognition of an issue with which to deal ('So let me think, how else could I have dealt with that situation? What might others say about it?')
- Emotion is involved in reflection, but emotion is involved in all learning. In deep reflection it is important to be aware of the impact of emotion on the quality of thinking.
- An important feature of reflection is its depth dimension. Superficial reflection is little different from description. It is deep reflection from which learning occurs. Therefore the courses must enable participants to understand what is meant by deep reflection and how it differs from superficial description.

The term 'reflective practice' is characterised by an attitude that there is always something to learn from adoption of regular and deliberate reflection. The aim will be the improvement of practice. The reflection may be in the medium of writing (e.g. in journals or on screens), or verbal – such as in deliberately structured conversations, through the use of 'critical friends' or support from a mentor.

A central feature of Courses A and B is the Graduated Scenario exercise. Such an exercise teaches what deep reflective writing looks like and illustrates the differences between effective (deep) reflection and poor (descriptive/superficial) writing from which less good learning is likely to take place. The Graduated Scenario exercise is based on critical incidents/stories and is practical and 'non-academic' and utilises discussion between participants rather than theoretical input. The learning that can emerge from it can be directly applied in a real-world situation (Moon, 2009).

Another feature of the course for coach educators was a block of material on the processes of how reflection relates to usual processes of learning and teaching in coach education. Observations from the literature and from conversations suggested that coach education may tend to be a didactic process of telling learners what it is felt they need to know with the expectation that they will 'absorb' the material uncritically. Such learning does not equip participants to deal with the 'messy' realities of the real coaching process. Such approaches tend to be antithetical to reflective learning.

Learning journals as a vehicle for reflection were introduced early on in Course A. Participants were expected to use learning journals during and between the sessions. It was in the proposed use of journals that some interesting attitudes to reflective learning emerged. There were sceptics who regarded journal writing as 'soft', while other participants celebrated their own experiences of use of journals. As well as the matter of differences in attitude to such practices, it is important also to recognise the reality that some people will 'get more' from reflective practices than others.

The 'Toolbox' was a section in the course handbook and it comprised a collection of ideas and exercises for the enhancement of reflective practice in the context of football. It is anticipated that it will also provide material for coach educators running Course B. Much of it is based on exercises in Moon (2006) – i.e. exercises that can be used as part of learning journal work. The Toolbox section of the booklet was introduced early in Course A.

In terms of the actual running of Course A, the first day included the following. Much of the material was introduced by way of active exercises rather than verbal presentation:

*   Reflection – what is it? What does it look like when written?
*   Understanding the notion of depth in reflection (Graduated Scenario).
*   The place of reflection in learning, teaching, coaching and training.
*   The sophistication of thinking (epistemological development).
*   The use of learning journals as a vehicle for reflection.
*   Introduction of the Toolbox.

After the first day-length session of Course A, the focus shifted more directly towards the development of Course B. It was vital that the participants of Course A should feel involved and confident in the planning of Course B. To develop that sense of involvement, in the second and third sessions there was introduction of a means of working that was developed originally for professional health educators (Moon & England, 1994). There was identification of specific issues that should be clarified in anticipation of development of Course B. These issues were presented on separate PowerPoint slides. For example, one was 'What should be the stated aims of Course B?' and another: 'What is the problem for coaches for which reflective learning is a solution?' Groups of four or five participants were asked to respond to such questions/issues as a group by writing a specified number of clear statements on a flip-chart sheet. Groups were given a strict and short length of time for the task (e.g. seven minutes). At the end of the time their responses were reviewed and the sheets of paper were collected for typing up and circulating. This process was productive, very active and it focused thought and produced material for the later planning of Course B.

Several ideas emerged during the work of the course. The most important was that the aim of the whole project at this stage should realistically be focused on the processes by which coaches learn from their coaching experience (i.e. learning from experience). It was recognised that the work would not, at present, relate so much to the initial coach education system. Changes there might come later, once a consistent view of reflective practice was adopted across the organisation (The FA).

As is indicated above, originally it was expected that participating coach educators would now move to develop and run Course B with coaches. However, now the plan is to run a three (full) day course on reflective practice, for all FA coach educators before the conduct of Course B sessions for coaches (Course A1). This will ensure that the whole of The FA as an organisation is utilising the same concepts and methods for facilitating reflective practice. The development of such consistency is one of the central aims of the project. It will mean that Course B will be run with greater perception of support and confidence. There will be variations in how the ideas of reflective practice are applied in Course B according to the levels and contexts of work of the coaches involved.

Implications

It was stated at the beginning of this chapter that prior to the institution of this project, The FA had already recognised the potential value of reflective practice and there were various references to it in FA literature and requirements to engage in it throughout The FA coach education materials. There was, however, inconsistency and evidence of superficiality in the manner in which such ideas were applied and taught. The 'Application of reflective practice' project was set up to build the consistency that was lacking and to institute a research-based approach to be instituted through continuing professional development (CPD) courses.

So what might be the implications of reflective practice for the behaviour of the individual coach in the context in which he works? A coach who engages in reflective practice will regularly take time to reflect, and take seriously the learning that can result from such reflection. He should become more thoughtful about his role as a coach and how he relates to the players, reviewing ideas around the performance of himself and players with more breadth and depth. He should learn better in the ways that coaches say they learn best – from experience. He is likely to come to understand better the role of prior experience in the determination of current behaviour and attitudes both of himself and of others. He will become more aware of how emotion impinges on decision-making and action and he is likely to be more able to talk about it. He is likely to be able to take a more listening, person-centred rather than didactic approach to coaching, becoming more approachable and more willing to accept that others might have a valuable contribution to his thinking on a particular matter. Active and overt engagement in reflective practice in coaching can encourage such practice in players and can have implications for those with other roles in The FA, such as referees.

There is much to learn from how this project has progressed so far. It has attempted to reform an area of action (reflective practice) in a group of people (coaches and coach educators) with specific roles with regard to others (players, other coaches) within the context of a large organisation which also requires to reformulate its approach to this practice to bring about confidence in and consistency of approach. These experiences from the project are those that might be relevant to any organisation wishing to institute reflective practice for its coaches and the educators of those coaches.

The project started with a recognition of a belief in the value of reflective practice, but also recognition of problems in its practice within the organisation. The external consultant employed for the project started in the project with a 'foot in both camps' of theory (in terms of books written on reflective learning) and practice (in running many courses on reflective learning with many different professions). In the process of development of the courses, it was essential to draw in practical football knowledge from others who were within the field and to then feed-in the theory through applied practical examples.

Sometimes it was better not to use football-related material in the development of generic ideas such as reflection. There is a tendency for participants to become caught up in the (in this case) footballing matters and fail to get the more general point that is being made. This particularly applied to the Graduated Scenarios, which are generic and have been used with many different professions. The decision of the developers of Course B is still that the generic form will be preferred.

It was also important to reflect on and to learn from the progress of the course itself. For example, some of the material in the course handbook was not used and alternative strategies were employed, in particular exercises in which intense discussions were stimulated by specific statements presented on PowerPoint slides (see above).

Another significant event in the progress of the project and courses has been the development of a sense of ownership of and confidence and expertise in the use of the materials for the cascading of the material to coaches within Course B. This process has been greatly facilitated by the emergence of the intermediate stage in which the coach educators selected for Course A will run courses for their own colleagues in coach education (Course A1) before the material is presented to all coaches. As has been said before, this additional process, not in the original plan, will facilitate much better adoption of a consistent and well-founded approach to reflective practice across the whole organisation of The FA. It will further enable or encourage other areas of football activity to engage in similar training – for example, the education of referees. It has already meant that reflective practice has become part of what coach educators do in their own educational practices.

In a project of this type, it is of course important to reflect on how well the project has gone – to assess its impact. In addition to the 'Application of reflective practice' project and the running of the courses, parallel work is planned by Bournemouth University (and agreed with The FA) to track and assess the impact of the work and outcomes of the project.

Critical questions

1. To what extent should reflective practices in whatever form chosen (journals, group discussion, etc.) be mandatory, or is it reasonable to recognise that they will work for some but not all coaches?
2. What is the best way to convince coaches that working at reflection is worthwhile? They may say that they reflect anyway.
3. How can a professional body keep a note of the quality of reflective practices of many thousands of individuals if it is to become an expected professional activity?
4. How are coaches to find time to reflect?

References

Abraham, A. & Collins, D. (1998). Examining and extending research in coach development. *Quest*, 50, 59–79.

Buysse, K., Sparkman, K. & Wesley, P. (2003). Communities of practice: connecting what we know with what we do. *Exceptional Children*, 69 (3), 263–277.

Carson, F. (2008). Utilizing video to facilitate reflective practice: developing sports coaches. *International Journal for Sport Science*, 3(3), 381–390.

Cushion, C., Armour, K. & Jones, R. (2003). Coach education and continuing professional development experience and learning to coach. *Quest*, 55, 215–230.

Demers, G., Woodburn, A. & Savard, C. (2006). The development of an undergraduate competency-based coach education programme. *The Sport Psychologist*, 20, 162–173.

Erikson, K., Cote, J. & Fraser-Thomas, J. (2007). Sport experiences, milestones and educational activities associated with high performance coaches' development. *The Sport Psychologist*, 21, 302–216.

Gilbert, W. & Trudel, P. (2001). Learning to coach through experience: reflection in model youth sport coaching, *Journal of Teaching in Physical Education*, 21, 16–24.

Gilbert, W. & Trudel, P. (2013). The role of deliberate practice in becoming an expert coach: Pt 2 reflection. *Olympic Coaching Magazine*, 24 (1), 35–44.

Harvey, S., Cushion, C. & Massa-Gonzalez, A. (2010). Learning a new method for understanding in the coach's eyes. *Physical Education and Sport Pedagogy*, 15 (4), 361–382.

Hughes, C., Lee, S. & Chesterfield, G. (2009). Innovation in sports coaching: the implementation of reflective cards. *Reflective Practice*, 10 (3), 367–384.

Jones, R. & Turner, P. (2006). Teaching coaches to coach holistically: can problem-based learning (PBL) help? *Physical Education and Sport Pedagogy*, 11 (2), 181–202.

Knowles, Z., Gilbourne, D., Borne, A. & Nevill, A. (2001). Developing the reflective sports coach: a study exploring the process of reflective practice within a higher education coaching programme. *Reflective Practice*, 2 (2), 185–207.

Knowles, Z., Tyler, G., Gilbourne, D. & Eubank, M. (2006). Reflecting on reflection: exploring the practice of sports coaching graduates. *Reflective Practice*, 7 (2), 163–179.

Kolb, D. (1984). *Experiential learning as the science of learning and development*. Englewood Cliffs, NJ: Prentice Hall.

Light, R. (2004). Coaches experience of 'Game Sense': opportunities and challenges. *Physical Education and Sport Pedagogy*, 90 (2), 115–131.

Moon, J. (1999a). *Reflection in learning and professional development*. London: Routledge.

Moon, J. (1999b). *Learning journals*. London: Routledge.

Moon, J. (2004). *A handbook of reflective and experiential learning*. London: Routledge.

Moon, J. (2006). *Learning journals: a handbook for reflective practice and professional development*. London: Routledge.

Moon, J. (2008). *Critical thinking: an exploration in theory and practice*. London: Routledge.

Moon, J. (2009). The use of graduated scenarios to facilitate the learning of complex and difficult-to-describe concepts in higher education. *Art and Design in Higher Education*, 8 (1), 57–70.

Moon, J. & England, P. (1994). Development of a highly structured workshop in health promotion. *Journal of Institute of Health Education*, 32 (2), 41–50.

Nash, C. & Sproule, J. (2009). Career development of expert coaches. *International Journal of Sport Science and Coaching*, 4 (1), 121–138.

Nelson, L. & Cushion, C. (2006). Reflection on coach education: the case of the National Governing Body Coaching Certificate. *The Sport Psychologist*, 20, 174–183.

Piggott, D. (2012). Coaches' experiences of formal coach education: a critical sociological experience. *Sport, Education and Society*, 17 (4), 535–554.

Potrac, P., Jones, R. & Armour, K. (2002). 'It's all about getting respect': the coaching behaviours of an expert English soccer coach. *Sport, Education and Society*, 7 (2), 183–202.

Roberts, S. (2011). Teaching games for understanding, the difficulties and challenges experienced by participation cricket coaches. *Physical Education and Sport Psychology*, 16 (1), 33–48.

Schon, D. (1987). *Educating Reflective Practitioners*. San Francisco, CA: Jossey-Bass.

Trudel, P. & Gilbert, W. (2013). The role of deliberate practice in becoming an expert coach: Pt 3 creating optimal settings. *Olympic Coach Magazine*, 24 (2), 15–28.

Trudel, P., Gilbert, W. & Werthner, P. (2010). Coach education effectiveness. In J. Lyle and C. Cushion (eds), *Sports coaching, professionalism and practice* (pp. 135–152). London: Elsevier.

Trudel, P., Culver, D. & Werthner, P. (2013). Looking at coach development from the coach learner's point of view. In P. Potrac, W. Gilbert & J. Dennison (eds), *Routledge handbook of sports coaching* (pp. 375–387). London: Routledge.

Turner, D., Nelson, L. & Potrac, P. (2012). The journey is the destination: reconsidering the expert sports coach. *Quest*, 64, 313–325.

Werthner, P. & Trudel, P. (2006). A new theoretical perspective for understanding how coaches learn to coach. *The Sport Psychologist*, 20, 198–212.

7

DELIVERING THE FA GRASSROOTS CLUB MENTOR PROGRAMME

Mentors' experiences of practice

Paul Potrac

Introduction

While there is no single clear and accepted conceptual definition, mentoring is largely understood to be 'a formalized process whereby a more knowledgeable and experienced person actuates a supportive role of overseeing and encouraging reflection and learning within a less experienced person, so as to facilitate that person's career and personal development' (Roberts, 2000: 162). Mentoring is, then, something that is done *with*, rather than *to*, a mentee, as well as being an investment in the total growth of the mentee (Jones *et al.*, 2009). Equally, it has been argued that, as mentoring is something that is personalised and heavily contextualised, it addresses Schon's (1987) call to work in the 'swamp of practice' better than many other educational strategies. Given these supposed benefits, it is perhaps unsurprising that formalised mentoring programmes have been increasingly adopted within the contexts of nursing, education and business (Jones *et al.*, 2009; Bloom, 2013), with the express intention of enhancing the skills, knowledge, creativity, resilience and understanding of employees at all levels of an organisation.

Such developments have, however, not been without criticism. Importantly, it has been suggested that many of the positive claims associated with mentoring provision are largely unfounded. For example, Colley (2003: 1) argued, 'existing research evidence scarcely justifies its use on such a scale, [while] the movement has not yet developed a sound theoretical basis to underpin policy or practice'. Indeed, despite its clear potential and the popularity of the rhetoric that accompanies it, we not only have a partial picture of what *tends* to happen in mentoring programmes and relationships, but also a limited understanding of the rich possibilities of what *could* happen (Jones *et al.*, 2009). Similarly, it has also been suggested that mentoring provision is often based upon rather simplistic understandings of empowerment. In this case, the mentor is seen as the powerful member of the mentor–mentee dyad based on his or her age and/or experience and the 'mentee as relatively powerless, awaiting benign empowerment by the benign actions of the mentor' (Colley, 2003: 139–140). Not only does this conceptualisation reify power as a commodity that is possessed and passed on by individuals, but it also ignores the messy and inherently social and relational realities of pedagogical interactions and relationships (Colley, 2003; Jones *et al.*, 2009). Indeed, we continue to know relatively little about how mentors might develop an appropriate mix of social, cultural and symbolic capital that allows them to obtain the 'buy-in', trust and respect of the mentee (Jones *et al.*, 2009). Given this state of affairs, there has been an increasing recognition of the need to move beyond superficial and one-dimensional accounts of this activity by better investigating the everyday realities of mentoring, especially in terms of the concerns, questions, reactions and coping strategies of all involved (Jones *et al.*, 2009; Bloom, 2013). It is believed that once such knowledge is generated, better-informed conceptualisations and recommendations for mentoring can be developed (Jones *et al.*, 2009; Bloom, 2013).

Similar to trends in other professions and occupations, the term mentoring has received increasing use within the language and practice of sports coaching and coach education. While mentoring has been increasingly positioned as a valuable educational tool for developing the knowledge and expertise of coaches in a variety of different sports (Jones, 2006; Jones *et al.*, 2009; Cushion and Nelson, 2013), it remains a little understood and under-researched topic of inquiry. In this regard, there remains considerable conceptual debate concerning mentoring (i.e. what it is), limited theorising related to the structure and delivery of mentoring provision (i.e. how it works) and, significantly, a paucity of empirical work that specifically addresses the experiences of mentors and mentees in the field (Jones *et al.*, 2009). With specific regard to the latter, it has been recommended that future inquiry into the mentoring of sports coaches should strive to generate empirical evidence related to the nature of the mentoring process, especially in terms of how it is experienced and understood by those involved at the micro level of social reality (Jones *et al.*, 2009). Indeed, it has been argued that, in order to avoid developing simplistic and overly sanitised accounts of mentoring, researchers and policy-makers in sports coaching ought to examine and better consider the 'dilemmas and nuances of mentoring relationships' (Jones *et al.*, 2009: 276), especially as they relate to the interactions between mentor, protégé and various others within coaching and coach education contexts. While the wider coaching literature has certainly begun to illuminate the complex nature of the pedagogical relationships that exist between coaches, athletes and other relevant contextual stakeholders (e.g. administrators, parents) in terms of their underpinning micropolitical dynamics (e.g. Potrac & Jones, 2009; Potrac *et al.*, 2013; Purdy *et al.*, 2013), such insights are not currently prevalent in relation to the work of coaching mentors.

FA case study research: key concepts

In 2013, The Football Association (The FA) introduced the Grassroots Club Mentor Programme. This innovative project seeks to achieve a variety of outcomes. These are:

- to support the development of coaches in grassroots football;
- to support The FA Vision and National Game Strategy (Better Players and Workforce Enabler);
- to support the delivery of The FA Coaching Strategy;
- to promote The FA *Future Game* philosophy.

The programme was initially delivered in a pilot format, with 56 mentors working with a variety of FA 'Charter Standard' clubs across England. The programme also provides a process whereby a coach is actively engaged in being guided towards acquiring new knowledge, feedback, ideas or advice by a trained mentor. The aim is to support a coaching workforce in their own environment, both in training and in match-day situations.

The purpose of this study was to investigate the mentors' subjective experiences of delivering The FA Grassroots Club Mentor Programme. Rather than setting out to evaluate the practice of individual mentors or, indeed, the mentoring programme as a whole, the goal of this study was to generate rich insights into the mentors' understandings of their participation in the scheme, especially in terms of their day-to-day interactions and working relationships with key contextual stakeholders (e.g. coach learners, players, club administrators and parents). A combination of in-depth, semi-structured interviews and an open-ended qualitative survey were used to achieve this goal (Nelson *et al.*, 2013). The combined interview and questionnaire data were analysed iteratively and the results of the study were organised around the following issues:

- the mentors' perspectives on establishing and managing relationships within the club setting;
- the mentors' experiences of the mentor–mentee relationship.

Establishing and managing relationships in the club setting

Generally, the mentors believed that they were welcomed into the various club settings in which the programme was delivered. This was especially so when the mentors had previously engaged with officials and/or coaches from the participating clubs. Here, for example, one coach noted:

> In terms of both clubs, I had already met key individuals like the secretary and chairman. I work with them quite a bit. I'd spoken to them about the mentoring programme at a club forum. They want to improve the club and are quite

open-minded, which helps. So I liaised with them and we organised a meeting for the coaches who wanted to participate in the mentoring programme.

However, this initial entry was not always a positive and straightforward process, as some mentors encountered coaches and club officials who were suspicious of The FA and the aims of the mentoring programme. In illustrating this point one mentor stated:

> clubs are difficult animals.... There are those that say, 'Yes, please help me.' And there are those that need help but will put up walls, be reticent, because 'I know football, it is opinions, what can you tell me?' ... There is some distrust of The FA in terms of telling people what to do, governance, fines and the like, so it's about explaining why I'm there and trying to chip down some of the barriers.

In attempting to address this situation, the mentors highlighted how they had to carefully engage with a number of individuals that they identified as key stakeholders within a club environment. This entailed a variety of formal and informal efforts to present themselves and the mentoring programme in a positive, empathetic and supportive manner. For example, one mentor noted:

> So I had to make sure that they realised why I was there. And breaking down the barriers and chipping them down took a few meetings.... I found the best way was to go straight in with club meetings, not to the mentees or potential mentees but into the club.... I am going to be totally honest and get it right in my head, probably six meetings for the two clubs to actually get started, so I think it was two at one and four at the other. But it was sitting down with the committee, explaining to the Charter Standard contact what it was about, how it was not going to cost them, how it is actually meaning to help, explaining that to the treasurer who couldn't make the first meeting.... So it was really kind of kid gloves to start with; support and explanation.

Despite the mentors making such efforts to obtain the 'buy-in' of club officials, there were, unfortunately, some occasions where the clubs have not appeared to respond in a positive or cooperative fashion. In illustrating this point, one mentor noted that:

> The other three coaches were with a professional club working in their local community. I got in touch with a contact I know there really well, explained that the project was about the three people that had been identified and could he help me with them and he never came back to me. I emailed him again – he never came back to me. I'm still waiting to get a reply to my phone calls, texts and email. It's certainly making me rethink how I view him. I'm going to spend my hours now working with one coach and then go back and try again with the club to get to work with those other three.

Interestingly, the mentees described mixed experiences of their engagements with, as well as support from, their local county football association in relation to the delivery of the programme. While many had generally positive encounters in this regard, some mentors experiences proved to be more problematic. For example, in illustrating this latter point, one mentor noted:

> I was in the middle of a presentation to the club and one county FA manager started to question me. He said 'But is it mentoring?' 'Sorry can you quantify?' 'It is not mentoring. Mentoring is just one to one that is what it is. I am an experienced mentor and mentoring is just a one to one relationship.' And it was, 'Right okay, I'm happy to speak to you about that afterwards' and there was about 50 people in the room. And, 'I know you are passionate about mentoring as I am, I am really looking forward to working with you. I have heard lots about your county and how much...' and he bristled a bit.... And I just had to again bite my lip, deal with the situation.... It was about him proving a point and saying, 'I am a county FA. It is my county you are coming into.' And he just needed to put a door in my face for a minute and ring fence his territory like they do and they make you step over a hurdle. Rather than come in and say 'How can we work together?' it is a case of 'make sure that you knock on my door before you come in'.

The mentors also described how, at times, they came to understand their work in the club setting to require them to sometimes engage with parents on an individual and collective basis. This was especially so when supporting mentee coaches to implement new practices and ideas. Here, one mentor noted:

> Obviously I have had the discussions with the individual parents and saying what they have been working on today and things like that. So I try to help the coach out a little bit and say, 'Yes they have been working on this, and he has done this and they have got this and they have improved on this' kind of things. Almost big-up the coach a little bit. A lot of the time the parents are just seeing them [the coach and players] on a Sunday when they are playing their matches. Often the parents are shouting and bawling and doing all those things that they do, as opposed to actually seeing what they [the coach and players] are working on in their training as well. So I try and give the coach that support.

Experiences of the mentor–mentee relationships

Many of the mentors highlighted how their engagements with the mentee coaches were a largely positive and rewarding part of their work. For example, one mentor stated:

I felt satisfaction and a sense of achievement. Also, I suppose, a sense of pride – not in myself but in the personal growth of the mentees. I suppose it was similar to seeing a player do something in a game that he had learnt in training. Overall, it has been great so far.

Interestingly, however, gaining the trust and respect of the mentees was not considered to be an unproblematic affair. Indeed, many of the mentors felt that they needed to 'prove' their knowledge and skills to the mentee coaches in order to obtain the latter's genuine 'buy-in' to the mentoring relationship. Here, the ability of the mentor to provide high-quality demonstration sessions in the club environment was considered to represent one possible means of achieving this outcome. For example, one mentor stated:

A lot of them have been saying, 'Well can you show me how to do this and how to do that?' And I think, with a couple of them in particular, it is probably a little bit of a test. It's like they're saying to me, 'Can you show me what you can do?' They've been involved in football for 20 years and think that I have nothing to offer them.... I did the practical session and it seemed to break down the barriers and I have built up really good relationships with them.... When I spoke to one of them after that session he said: 'It was great! The kids were buzzing when they came off'.... So from then on he was on board because of the feedback he had from the kids. They had enjoyed it and he had seen their reaction to it. So from then onwards he started giving me the 'time of day'.

In addition, the mentors also described how some of the barriers that they considered to exist between them and the mentees could sometimes be ameliorated by their being seen to understand a mentee 'as a person' as much as a coach. Here, for example, one mentor noted:

Generally the coach didn't seem very comfortable with me observing him. I could see that his son was a bit of a pain in the sessions. I tried my best to feedback in a positive and constructive way, but we just didn't seem to be connecting.... So with him, I had a really good open chat about a lot of things other than coaching football.... And he told me some of the problems he had at home with his son and some of his personal issues. His son's behaviour was straining his relationships with some of the other kids and their parents. It was obviously something that he was worried about when I was around, and I think him telling me those things got a weight off his shoulders. I explained again that I wasn't there to judge him or criticise. I want to help. I think that was a big breakthrough and good for his peace of mind.

Importantly, the mentors described how the adoption of various interactional strategies, such as those outlined above, could contribute to bringing about positive change in terms of a mentee coach's knowledge, reasoning and practice. In illustrating this point, one mentor noted that:

> Once I felt that I had them feeling comfortable to work with me, we made some really good strides together.... [For example] the coaches used the Youth Award Module 1 'Skills Corridor' where every player was challenged appropriately, with passing/dribbling/goalkeeping going on in the same practice, but with different levels of difficulty. It was a real 'light bulb' moment for them on how to get technical work done in an enjoyable way, without lines or queues, and catering for everyone. They could see the benefits of what we had been working on.

Despite such successes, the mentors expressed a concern regarding what would happen in the club once the mentoring time allocation had been fulfilled. In particular, several of the mentors were concerned that the mentees' progress could be undermined by interactions and relationships with various stakeholders in the club that both pre-dated, and would continue after, the mentor's departure from the club environment. For example, one mentor stated:

> I wonder what will happen at the club when my hours are up. The coaches I've worked with have certainly come on but I don't think they have the skills or strength of character to push through some of the changes that we've made with them in that club environment. You wonder what the long-term legacy will be.

Of course, as with all pedagogical relationships, the mentors sometimes experienced persistent difficulties in terms of a mentee's willingness to engage with them in a constructive manner. It was believed that such occurrences could be largely understood in relation to a mentee's fear about developing and changing existing coaching beliefs and practices. Indeed the mentors felt that some mentees were not only worried about their ability to change, but also the negative reactions that they might receive from others in the club environment when attempting to coach in new or different ways. For example, one mentor noted that:

> It's frustrating when it happens, but I think sometimes the thought of changing what they do is too much for some people. You know, change is a scary thing for them. It's easier to stick with what they know and are comfortable with. One mentee said that some of the parents had been critical of his experimentations with some of the practices that we had worked on. You could tell he wasn't happy. He was used to getting positive feedback from them and this really rocked him. From then on he made excuses for why it was probably best that he should stick with what he thought was best.

Implications for NGBs

While the mentors' engagements and relationships with others in the club setting were frequently positive and constructive affairs, they were not entirely unproblematic. At various times, many of the mentors experienced a variety of tensions and challenges both directly in their dealings with club officials and mentee coaches, as well as indirectly in terms of some parents' reactions to the coaching practices of the mentees. Given these initial findings, national governing bodies (NGBs) may wish to consider how they respectively facilitate coach educators' and mentors' engagement with issues such as their noticing (e.g. ability to notice and anticipate the actions and reactions of others), impression management, persuasion and conflict management skills in both their induction programmes and subsequent CPD opportunities. While the technical and procedural features of the mentor and coach educator job role certainly should not be underestimated, such skills and knowledge should not be seen to exist outside of the demands, dilemmas and dramas of organisational life (Thompson *et al.*, 2013; Huggan *et al.*, 2015). One way to broach and explore such topics in coach education provision is the sharing of mentors' and coach educators' stories as narrative resources (Smith & Sparkes, 2009). In this way, neophyte practitioners, for example, may come to better appreciate the socio-cultural and relational dynamics of their respective working environments than has traditionally been the case.

The stance to coach education advocated above is in keeping with recent developments in the coaching literature (e.g. Chesterfield *et al.*, 2010; Jones *et al.*, 2013; Huggan *et al.*, 2015; Potrac & Jones, 2009) that have increasingly explored coaching and coach education through a micropolitical lens. Such work is based upon the premise that politics is a generalised feature of social life and exists whenever two or more people engage in any form of collective action (Leftwhich, 2005). In the context of sports coaching, the roots of such micropolitical inquiry lie in an increasing dissatisfaction with the largely functional and apolitical representations of organisational life that have predominated in the literature and educational provision to date (Jones *et al.*, 2011; Nelson *et al.*, 2014).

In drawing upon the work of pioneering scholars such as Ball (1987) and Kelchtermans (2009, 2011), coaching researchers have, at last, shed some light on the ways in which everyday occurrences such as disagreements about purposes, practices and the deployment of resources can trigger strategic actions, as individuals and groups seek to gain control of emerging situations (Jones *et al.*, 2011). Indeed, while the study of micropolitics in the coaching literature is at an embryonic stage of development, it has arguably begun to highlight the limitations of viewing organisational life in sports clubs and organisations as only being characterised by coherent and cohesive social relationships and networks or, instead, as settings where openness, trust and rationality exclusively prevail. Recent studies (e.g. Potrac & Jones, 2009; Huggan *et al.*, 2015; Purdy & Jones, 2011; Purdy *et al.*, 2013; Thompson *et al.*, 2013) have examined the importance that coaches, athletes and performance analysts attach to obtaining, maintaining and advancing the 'buy-in' and support that they receive from key contextual stakeholders to be a critical feature of their working lives and practices.

By way of illustrating the points made above, Potrac and Jones (2009) considered the experiences and practices of Gavin, a newly appointed head coach at a semi-professional football club, as he sought to gain acceptance and 'buy-in' from the players, as well as displace a dysfunctional assistant coach who threatened his agenda. Gavin's thoughts and actions not only focused on developing and re-forging relationships with various contextual stakeholders, but also the engagement in considerable 'face-work' (Goffman, 1959). With regard to the latter, Gavin explained how he carefully considered and managed the impression of himself that he gave to others in his efforts to manage them towards desired ends. Importantly, the findings such have these have suggested that an individual coach's relationships with various contextual stakeholders may not only influence the time, space and resources that are afforded to an individual, but also the climate in which he or she attempts to fulfil stated objectives and goals. Arguably, the exploration of such social dynamics within the contexts of mentoring and coach education may enable us to develop a knowledge base that is grounded in the nuanced realities of practice (Jones & Wallace, 2005; Jones et al., 2011).

In closing, it is suggested that a continued reluctance to engage with the liberating and constraining effects of micropolitical tensions, actions and discord in the specific contexts of mentoring and coach education only serves to reinforce a distorted and overly utopian view of these activities; where they are devoid of their essential social and relational complexities (Jones et al., 2013; Nelson et al., 2013; Potrac & Jones, 2009). As such, coach education may, from both academic and practical perspectives, benefit from a greater consideration of the ways in which coaches, mentors and coach educators are (always) engaged in networks of learning, influence and practice that extend beyond the dyadic relationship that exists between educator and learner or mentor and mentee (Crossley, 2011). Indeed, it is, arguably, time for coach education research to consider how individuals' thoughts, feelings and actions are not only consciously 'oriented to other actions within the network' in which they are embedded, but also 'the opportunities and constraints afforded' to them within their particular networks of coaching and coach education relationships (Crossley, 2011: 2).

Critical questions

1. Why are sports clubs and coaching environments largely represented as apolitical arenas in coach education provision?
2. In what ways might conceptualising coaching and mentoring as socially and emotionally sterile activities limit coach education and development provision?
3. What are some of the possible shortcomings of only viewing mentoring work to consist of the interactions and relationships that occur between the mentor and the mentee?

4. How might we best prepare mentors and coach educators to gain the trust and 'buy-in' of those they engage with?
5. How might the issues of resistance and organisational misbehaviour be productively explored in coach education provision?

References

Ball, S. (1987). *The micropolitics of the school: towards a theory of school organization*. London: Methuen.

Bloom, G. (2013). Mentoring for sports coaches. In P. Potrac, W. Gilbert & J. Denison (eds), *The Routledge handbook of sports coaching*. London: Routledge.

Chesterfield, G., Potrac, P. & Jones, R. (2010). Studentship and impression management in an advanced soccer coach education award. *Sport, Education,and Society*, 15 (3), 299–314.

Colley, H. (2003). *Mentoring for social inclusion: a critical approach to nurturing mentor relationships*. London: Routledge.

Crossley, N. (2011). *Towards relational sociology*. London: Routledge.

Cushion, C. & Nelson, L. (2013). Coach education and learning: developing the field. In P. Potrac, W. Gilbert & J. Denison (eds), *The Routledge handbook of sports coaching*. London: Routledge.

Goffman, E. (1959). *The presentation of the self in everyday life*. London: Penguin Books.

Huggan, R., Nelson, L. & Potrac, P. (2015). Developing micropolitical literacy in professional football: a performance analyst's tale. *Qualitative Research in Sport, Exercise, and Health*, 7 (4), 504–520.

Jones, R. (2006). *The sports coach as educator: re-conceptualising sports coaching*. London: Routledge.

Jones, R. & Wallace, M. (2005). Another bad day at the training ground: coping with ambiguity in the coaching context. *Sport, Education, and Society*, 10 (1), 119–134.

Jones, R., Harris, R. & Miles, A. (2009). Mentoring in sports coaching: a review of the literature. *Physical Education and Sport Pedagogy*, 14 (3), 267–284.

Jones, R., Potrac, P., Cushion, C., & Ronglan, L.T. (2011). *The sociology of coaching*. London: Routledge.

Jones, R., Bailey, J. & Thompson, A. (2013). Ambiguity, noticing and orchestration: further thoughts on managing the complex coaching context. In P. Potrac, W. Gilbert & J. Dennison (eds), *The Routledge handbook of sports coaching*. London: Routledge.

Kelchtermans, G. (2009). Who I am in how I teach is the message: self-understanding, vulnerability and reflection. *Teachers and Teaching: Theory and Practice*, 15 (2), 257–272.

Kelchtermans, G. (2011). Vulnerability in teaching: the moral and political roots of a structural condition. In C. Day & K. Lee (eds), *New understandings of teacher's work*. Netherlands: Springer.

Leftwhich, A. (2005). The political approach to human behavior: people, resources and power. In A. Leftwhich (ed.), *What is politics?* Cambridge: Polity Press.

Nelson, L., Cushion, C.J. & Potrac, P. (2013). Enhancing the provision of coach education: the recommendations of UK coaching practitioners. *Physical Education and Sport Pedagogy*, 18 (2), 204–218.

Nelson, L., Potrac, P., Gilbourne, D., Allanson, A., Gale, L. & Marshall, P. (2014). Thinking, feeling, acting: the case of a semi-professional soccer coach. *Sociology of Sport Journal*, 19 (1), 19–40.

Potrac, P. & Jones, R. (2009). Micro-political workings in semi-professional football coaching. *Sociology of Sport Journal*, 26, 557–577.

Potrac, P., Jones, R., Gilbourne, D. & Nelson, L. (2013). Handshakes, BBQs, and bullets: a tale of self-interest and regret in football coaching. *Sports Coaching Review*, 1 (2), 79–92.

Purdy, L. & Jones, R. (2011). Choppy waters: elite rowers' perceptions of coaching. *Sociology of Sport Journal*, 28 (3), 329–346.

Purdy, L., Potrac, P. & Nelson, L. (2013). Trust, distrust and coaching practice. In P. Potrac, W. Gilbert & J. Denison (eds), *The Routledge handbook of sports coaching*. London: Routledge.

Roberts, A. (2000). Mentoring revised: a phenomenological reading of the literature. *Mentoring and Tutoring: Partnership in Learning*, 8 (2), 145–169.

Schon, D. (1987). *Educating the reflective practitioner: towards a new design for teaching and learning in the professions*. San Francisco, CA: Jossey-Bass Inc.

Smith, B. & Sparkes, A. (2009). Narrative analysis and sport and exercise psychology: understanding lives in diverse ways. *Psychology of Sport and Exercise*, 10 (2), 279–288.

Thompson, A., Potrac, P. & Jones, R. (2013). 'I found out the hard way': micro-political workings in professional football. *Sport, Education and Society*. doi: 10.1080/13573322. 2013.862786.

PART III
Impact and practice

8

WHAT DO COACHES LEARN AND CAN NEW KNOWLEDGE BE EFFECTIVELY APPLIED?

Eleanor Quested, Paul Appleton and Joan Duda

Introduction

From grassroots to elite football contexts, the quality of young players' sporting experience is recognised to be critical to sustained participation as well as the extent to which players maximise their capabilities and realise wellbeing when playing the sport. The coach and the environment he/she creates are recognised to be central determinants of whether young footballers' participation is more or less positive or maladaptive. Consequently, coaches are encouraged to engage in training in order to learn how they can maximise their role and responsibilities when interacting with their players.

For several years, research has substantiated that establishing and maintaining quality motivation is the cornerstone for any coach to achieve his or her objectives, regardless of whether those objectives include optimising the enjoyment experienced by a nine-year-old grassroots player or winning a major international tournament. 'Motivation' is a frequently used but often misunderstood term in coaching contexts (Duda & Pensgaard, 2002). Motivation is often considered to exist as a quantitative element. That is, coaches might often consider that a player can be judged as high or low in motivation, evidenced via the level and direction of effort, interest and engagement exerted towards a task. As such, coaches may use a range of tactics in an effort to increase levels of motivation (Appleton *et al.*, 2016). However, according to well supported theoretical perspectives on motivation (e.g. Deci & Ryan, 2000; Nicholls, 1989) and an array of research in football and other team sports (see Quested & Duda, 2011 for a review), it is important to consider not only how much motivation a player has but also the quality of the players' motivation. Reasons and motives to engage in an activity such as football are sometimes autonomous (i.e. for fun, to learn, develop and accomplish, to reach personal goals and standards of achievement) and sometimes controlled (i.e. due to personal or external pressures, to gain praise or avoid punishment or for acclaim, fame and rewards). Evidence suggests that only those more autonomous motives are likely to sustain for the long term and be good for the development and wellbeing of the player. Coaches have the potential to optimise players' motivation via the coaching climate they create (Duda, 2001; Duda & Balaguer, 2007).

Theories of motivation (i.e. the achievement goal frameworks and self-determination theory (SDT): Ames, 1992; Nicholls, 1989; Deci & Ryan, 2000) describe the key dimensions of the climate created by significant others (such as coaches) pertinent to participants' engagement, as well as their motivational and health-related correlates. Pulling from research underpinned by both of these theories, Duda (2013) has recently proposed that the motivational climate can be considered to be characterised by more or less empowering and/or disempowering features. According to this perspective, only more empowering climates will foster more autonomous and sustained motivation among players. More empowering coaches tend to coach, communicate and relate to players in a way that is more likely to lead them to feel a sense of autonomy (i.e. that the players have a feeling of voice and choice, input and control over their football enjoyment), to feel competent (i.e. that they have the skills and attributes to be effective in their game) and to feel connected (i.e. cared for, respected and valued) to the coach and others in the team. On the contrary, when a coach is displaying disempowering behaviours, players are more likely to feel controlled and limited in voice and choice, incompetent and ineffective, and lonely, isolated and even rejected by the coach and others in the team. In the latter environment, players are more likely to play football for controlled reasons. As a consequence, these players will have a more negative football experience and will be more at risk of dropout, burnout and other indicators of ill-being.

While existent coach education programmes may acknowledge the important role of motivation and the environments that coaches create, this content tends to be limited in depth and not tied to our understanding of key processes within contemporary theoretical frameworks nor grounded in existent scientific evidence. The evidence-based Empowering Coaching™ programme pulls from and integrates key concepts within the aforementioned theories (as well as principles of behavioural change) and focuses on promoting coaches' understanding of the determinants of quality motivation and, importantly, their more effective application of strategies geared towards having young athletes feel more autonomous, competent and connected within their sport.

The recent 'PAPA' project (www.projectpapa.org; Duda et al., 2013) has generated a substantial database concerning the prevailing features of the motivational climate (i.e. how empowering, how disempowering) created by coaches in grassroots football in England (and across four other countries) and key player outcomes associated with variability in perceived and objectively rated coach behaviours. Via this large-scale European Commission-funded research project, more information was also obtained regarding grassroots coaches' attempts to implement the learned principles from the Empowering Coaching™ workshop, and the subsequent impact upon players' intentions to continue/drop out of the sport and their wellbeing. Qualitative research (Quested *et al.*, 2011) has revealed that the education programme positively impacted upon the coaches' practices when coaching and led to an amalgamation of Empowering Coaching™ principles within their personal coaching philosophy. Grassroots coaches also indicated that they employed reflective practice and drew from workshop resources to facilitate implementation of Empowering Coaching™ strategies 'on the pitch'.

In addition to these important findings, research is required to verify that a change in coach knowledge has occurred as a function of attendance at the Empowering Coaching™ workshop, particularly in the case of experienced (expert) coaches. Moreover, evidence is needed to examine whether there is a link between newly acquired knowledge (as a function of attending the Empowering Coaching™ programme) and experienced/expert coaches' ability to effectively apply this knowledge (in a manner that is truly aligned with the underlying theoretical principles). Such information would provide further evidence regarding the added value of Empowering Coaching™ as a means to enhance coaches' knowledge base and behaviours above and beyond what is possible via existing coach education programmes. Such evidence regarding added value would be particularly telling if the coaches in question are more experienced and already quite 'well trained' in terms of completed coaching awards.

FA case study research: key concepts

This chapter describes a recent research project intended to specifically delineate the added value of the Empowering Coaching™ educational workshop in terms of: (1) experienced/expert coaches' understanding of principles of effective motivation, and (2) experienced/expert understanding of how and which coaching behaviours impact young players' motivation and the quality of their experiences in the sport. This project was designed to provide an in-depth exploration of the degree to which a selected group of experienced FA coaches can understand, and then interpret and effectively apply, the principles of more empowering coaching (Duda, 2013).

Aims

The aims of the project were to explore:

*   how experienced coaches' knowledge base regarding the concepts of motivation, the motivational climate and what makes for effective coaching practice changes as a result of attending the Empowering Coaching™ workshop;
*   differences before and after the workshop in how these experienced coaches apply knowledge and principles of quality motivation.

Methodology

Participants and procedure

Seven coaches with an average of 13.43 ($\pm$ 4.31) years of coaching experience participated in the project. The coaches fulfilled a range of roles in The FA at grassroots, regional and national levels. Once ethical approval had been secured, coaches attended individual interviews lasting an average of 51 minutes at the first time point (time one; T1). Interviews followed a guide that included a series of specific questions designed to target the project themes, including coaches' knowledge base concerning the motivational climate, motivation and the strategies they and other coaches may use to effectively (or ineffectively) motivate players. Interviews were filmed and audio recorded and subsequently transcribed verbatim. Approximately two months later, the coaches attended the six-hour Empowering Coaching™ workshop. A month later, coaches were re-interviewed (time two; T2) to examine changes from pre- to post-workshop. Questions also tapped the coaches' perceptions of the value of and need for the Empowering Coaching™ workshop in terms of coach education. These interviews lasted an average of 58 minutes. A deductive content analysis procedure reviewed the meaning in the text and assigned units of text to exemplify change that had occurred from pre- to post-workshop in relation to the pre-determined categories inherent to the research aims.

Results

A summary of the results is presented in the form of a detailed and rich narrative summary, with exemplar quotes reflecting the themes central to the study aims.

Changes in coaches' understanding of key terms

The Empowering Coaching™ workshop is a theory-based programme. As such, specific words and phrases have precise definitions and the coaches' understanding of these concepts is critical to the degree to which the coaches are then able to effectively operationalise ('bring to life') the embedded notions/principles in their coaching. Within the workshop, the coaches are challenged to reconsider their understanding and interpretation of key terms (e.g. motivation, motivational climate, autonomy) in the context of contemporary theories.

Pre-workshop understanding of 'motivation'

There was a mix in the level, sophistication and accuracy of the coaches' understanding of the key term of 'motivation' prior to the workshop. There was evidence that some coaches had previously studied and/or been exposed to the overall topic of motivation. All coaches took a multidimensional perspective to define motivation ('in terms of motivation, it's two fold, either intrinsic motivation or extrinsic motivation, and, I think no matter what sport you're in, you would see examples of both in a person' – coach #64, female, T1). However, not all coaches used the terms 'intrinsic' and 'extrinsic' to refer to different types of motivation. Prior to the workshop there was a tendency for the coaches to also use more antiquated definitions of motivation ('the direction of your actions and the intensity of those actions, I would say' – coach #66, male, T1) or not effectively differentiate the meaning between key terms such as arousal, confidence and motivation.

Post-workshop understanding of 'motivation'

In the interviews after the workshop, the overarching concept of 'motivation' was described by the coaches more precisely and accurately. There was evidence that this concept and related terms were now understood in the context of theory and in relation to other key variables ('The biggest thing really that I took away, was around developing intrinsic motivation to ensure that kids have autonomy, belonging and competence, as a real key facet of everything that we do' – coach #62, male, T2). The coaches also now demonstrated that they understood the potentially negative impact of using rewards and praise on intrinsic interest ('it is important to, to reward children, because we all like rewards, but it's the reasoning behind it would be then more beneficial ... [it has to be based on] realistic goals, their ability to do it ... to keep their behaviour as well' – coach #63, female, T2).

Pre-workshop understanding of 'motivational climate'

The coaches tended to make reference to positive and negative coaching environments without honing in on the relevant motivational qualities of those environments, or interpreting them in relation to implications for player motivation. The coaches were aware that the motivational climate they create is critical ('A very wise man once said to me, they, children, and, and well, generally people turn up 100 per cent motivated. So the first rule of motivation is don't demotivate.' – coach #66, male, T1). However, the coaches didn't necessarily capture the 'what, how or why' in terms of the motivational climate. In other words, they did not acknowledge the specific contents and/or mechanisms by which the coach-created environment impacts players' motivation and engagement in football.

Post-workshop understanding of 'motivational climate'

At T2 the coaches' wording and overall understanding when describing the coaching climate had evolved and captured fundamental themes central to the workshop:

> [an empowering climate is] creating an environment where they, people, athletes, players, whatever you want to refer to them as, they, are involved,

actively involved in the process, engaged in the process, and they feel they have some sort of ownership over what's going on, and they're learning as well.

(Coach #66, male, T2)

It was noteworthy that at T2 many of the behaviours/perspectives that we would interpret as critical to more empowering coaching (and thus, aligned with contemporary thinking regarding optimal motivational processes) were more specifically described and integrated into the responses (categorised below), reflecting the coaches' more astute understanding of effective practice.

Effective practice

Pre-workshop comments regarding what constitutes effective and ineffective practice

Prior to the workshop, it was clear that the coaches' perceptions of effective practice reflected coaching philosophies that were primarily player-centred ('Holistic development of the kids. Football is that vehicle to develop better people' – coach #62, male, T1). Coaches made reference to what they considered markers of effective ('That all the kids come back; help them get better at football; the winning stuff is kind of, neither here nor there to me' – coach #62, male, T1) as well as successful ('Long term would be to see them at age 11, in a grassroots team, enjoying football, making new friends. Technically better players, allowing them to kind of, express themselves with a ball' – coach #63, female, T1) and unsuccessful ('If I am that coach that stops a kid playing football, because of the environment I create, and I have, then I'll need to go and do something else, I've failed' – coach #62, male, T1] coaching behaviours.

Five of the coaches' views made reference to effective practice being reflected in making football enjoyable ('no matter what sport it is that you're coaching, that those young people come away with a love of whatever sport that is' – coach #64, female, T1), encouraging the players to make friends, allowing them to express themselves with the ball – and the link to sustained participation. Another coach expressed that effective practice was about promoting interest, but fun and enjoyment were the priority ('mainly, keep it interesting for the children, erm, let them have fun … experiment, but most of all have fun and enjoyment'). One coach referred to team and individual competition as being part of effective coaching:

> I think competition is a big part of it, again, not the end product of winning the medals or trophies, but it could be just gaining team points. So team games with competitions, is a big motivation factor … it's realising the ability levels to what that child needs to motivate themselves.
>
> *(Coach #63, female, T1)*

But at T1 this coach was not able to clearly explain the mechanisms as to how to integrate competition into effective coaching, particularly via what would be considered an 'empowering' manner.

All of the coaches were also able to talk at length about what they considered ineffective coaching practice and these examples often related to what we would call more disempowering, controlling approaches to coaching ('the coach that goes from, "oi, don't do that" to "right you're now sitting out", there's got to be somewhere in the middle ground for those strategies to deal with supporting the motivation' – coach #62, male, T1). At T1, however, on the whole, the coaches tended to be able to describe ineffective behaviour but not necessarily articulate and qualify the motivational limitations of the behaviour.

Post-workshop comments regarding what constitutes effective and ineffective practice

Post-workshop, the coaches explained more specifically and accurately the mechanisms that underpinned whether a coaching practice was effective or not. In general, the coaches' interpretation of what constituted markers of effective and successful coaching tended to be consistent with their T1 standpoints. However, their understanding of how they and other coaches can be more effective was more developed in what they expressed at T2. In particular, six of the seven coaches' comments more overtly and directly linked to effective coaching behaviours that supported the basic psychological needs of players (i.e. the key determinants of quality motivation and optimal functioning, namely players' feelings of autonomy, task-involved competence and relatedness):

> I look at myself as a coach and am I supporting the players' needs? I then look away from football … can we then socially kind of bond a little bit more, so that, come a Sunday for example, it's not all about the results last week, it could be we had a great time on Thursday doing whatever, and that would be the topic of conversation which would … feel at ease for more players that it's not [all about] a big, big result.
>
> *(Coach #63, female, T2)*

Four coaches also demonstrated an increased self-awareness and recognition of when previous coaching practice may have been ineffective due to its 'disempowering' features:

> I would imagine, over my coaching time I would have done some things that… I didn't realise the knock on effect of that, that would obviously disempower children or other coaches … for example, sometimes the environment that I set for them was very kind of, command style, erm, maybe to gain respect, erm, and the important thing for me as I was starting out was, I'd like people to respect me as a coach, so it's almost that

authoritativeness, erm, and that copycat culture of, well I've seen other coaches who are like this so I'm gonna do it, and then as it's evolved.

(Coach #63, female, T2)

Implications

This project has implications at a number of levels. With regard to the implications for the coaches themselves, within the follow-up interview we explored coaches' perceptions that the Empowering Coaching™ workshop had modified their current practice. The coaches provided a number of comments in regard to how their practice(s) has changed as a result of participating in the workshop. Examples were given of practical ways of coaching that differed to what the coaches had done previously:

I give them a voice, an opinion, of what to do next maybe in the session, or how they find the session, give them then a chance to change the session. Purposely I might kind of put something in the session so that they have a problem to solve.

(Coach #63, female, T2)

Some of the changes reported were recognised to be subtle:

I think it's the little subtleties, for me it's little subtle changes, or little, little subtle, pieces of information that I wouldn't have said last time [T1] … I don't know that it would have been significantly noticeable on behalf of the people in front of me, but that's probably a good thing. You wouldn't want them to go in and think, 'Oh my God this person is so radical and off the wall, that it makes me uncomfortable.'

(Coach #64, female, T2)

Examples were also provided in terms of fostering players' sense of belonging:

All I'm doing is making, notes, of subtle conversations that I'm having with individual players, what are their hobbies, what are their interests, who do they support, who's their favourite player, and it's, it's not an interview style, it's just casual conversation, and trying to, understand them, holistically, rather than just look at them as players, on a chalk board.

(Coach #66, male, T2)

Reference was also made to how the coaches' approach to planning sessions changed as a function of participation in the workshop ('I would say it's certainly affected the, the planning more so than anything else, but obviously you've got to reflect in action, and, in working you, you have to do something to help the kids' – coach #62, male, T2). As revealed across the two interviews, there were also observed changes in elements of self-awareness and in interpretation of the coaches' current and past behaviours:

> [before the workshop] I wouldn't have said me dictating a learning goal…. I wouldn't have seen that as dictating, I would have seen that as someone being really prepared as a coach, that's planned thoroughly to ensure that learning happens. Whereas when you look at it in terms of a, like a, empowering climate perspective, it's actually, quite a negative controlling thing to do, and then you link that back to those videos that you showed us, you actually demonstrate that climate really well, in terms of that process.
>
> *(Coach #64, female, T2)*

Findings also have implications for the potential for the Empowering Coaching™ workshop to add value to the current FA coach education system. These findings are summarised below:

- The T1 baseline data suggest that the coaches within the targeted sample had an appreciation of what is important and what are adaptive considerations when creating a positive motivational environment with young players.
- At T1 and T2, the coaches demonstrated an understanding of some motivation-related strategies, such as goal setting, and how to support players in setting specific goals for training and matches.
- While coaches recognised the importance of motivation to effective coaching, the T1 results suggest that this understanding was superficial and, at times, not always aligned with contemporary and scientifically grounded perspectives on the topic.
- At T1, the coaches were less able to effectively (i.e. concretely and/or accurately) describe specific mechanisms that may lead a particular coach behaviour to have a 'positive' or 'negative' impact upon players.
- Overall, the follow-up T2 (post-workshop) interviews suggested that the coaches developed a more sophisticated, accurate and theory-based understanding of what constitutes and supports healthy, adaptive motivation in young players. That is, following participation in the Empowering Coaching™ workshop, the coaches referred more to the particular processes by which coaches influence the motivation and welfare/functioning of their players.
- At T2 the coaches utilised more theoretically grounded concepts and mechanisms to give meaning and more developed interpretations to the video stimuli and their own examples of adaptive and maladaptive coach behaviours.
- At T2 coaches identified a range of ways that the workshop had positively impacted their planning and delivery of coaching and tutoring.
- Several coaches indicated that the Empowering Coaching™ workshop would add to the current coach education offered by The FA.

In sum, findings highlight the potential added value of Empowering Coaching™ for this sample of more experienced coaches (and tutors) working within The FA. It is reasonable to expect (and evidence from the PAPA project supports this prediction) that the impact of workshop participation on grassroots and/or less well trained (in terms of courses/coaching awards completed) football coaches would be even more pronounced. All coaches interviewed commented that Empowering Coaching™ would add value to the current FA provision of coach education. The coaches expressed views that the inclusion of the Empowering Coaching™ workshop is warranted in programme offerings across the spectrum of coaching levels.

This project also has implications for future research. For example, this project was undertaken with a sample of experienced coaches who hold various managerial/tutor/leadership roles within FA coach education and have had previous education within some of the overall topics targeted within Empowering Coaching™. Replication of the project among coaches with different levels of exposure to coach education and years of coaching experience (including coaches in the professional game) would be of interest. In addition, the time frame for this project was short, with only a month post-workshop for the coaches to report attempted changes to their behaviour. It would be informative to undertake such a study over a longer period of time or with repeated interviews to further elucidate the processes of behaviour change. This study could also be effectively complemented with objective observation of coaches, to ascertain the effect of the Empowering Coaching™ workshop on their overt behaviour in training and matches.

Critical questions

1. What are the characteristics of empowering and disempowering motivational climates and how do these climates relate to motivation?
2. What evidence was found of changes in the coaches' understanding of the key concepts?
3. What changes occurred in the coaches' behaviour following attendance at the workshop?
4. What are the 'take home' messages for the future of coach education?

References

Ames, C. (1992). Achievement goals and adaptive motivational patterns: the role of the environment. In G.C. Roberts (ed.), *Motivation in sport and exercise* (pp. 161–176). Champaign, IL: Human Kinetics.

Appleton, P., Ntoumanis, N., Quested, E., Viladrich, C. & Duda, J.L. (2016). Initial validation of the coach-created Empowering and Disempowering Motivational Climate Questionnaire (EDMCQ-C). *Psychology of Sport and Exercise*, 22, 53–65.

Deci, E.L. & Ryan, R.M. (2000). The 'what' and 'why' of goal pursuits: human needs and the self-determination of behaviour. *Psychological Inquiry*, 11, 227–268.

Duda, J.L. (2001). Achievement goal research in sport: pushing the boundaries and clarifying some misunderstandings. In G.C. Roberts (ed.), *Advances in motivation in sport and exercise* (pp. 129–182). Leeds: Human Kinetics.

Duda, J.L. (2013). The conceptual and empirical foundations of Empowering Coaching™: setting the stage for the PAPA project. *International Journal of Sport and Exercise Psychology*, 11 (4), 311–318.

Duda, J.L. & Balaguer, I. (2007). The coach-created motivational climate. In S. Jowett & D. Lavalee (eds), *Social psychology of sport* (pp. 117–130). Champaign, IL: Human Kinetics.

Duda, J.L. & Pensgaard, A.L. (2002). Enhancing the quantity and quality of motivation: the promotion of task involvement in a junior football team. In I. Cockerill (ed.), *Solutions in sport psychology* (pp. 49–57). London: Thomson Learning.

Duda, J.L., Quested, E., Haug, E., Samdal, O., Wold, B., Balaguer, I., Castillo, I., Sarrazin, P., Papaioannou, A., Ronglan, L.-T., Cruz, J. & Hall, H.K. (2013). Promoting adolescent health through an intervention aimed at improving the quality of their participation in physical activity (PAPA): background to the project and main trial protocol. *International Journal of Sport and Exercise Psychology*, 11 (4), 319–327.

Nicholls, J.G. (1989). *The competitive ethos and democratic education.* Cambridge, MA: Harvard University Press.

Quested, E. & Duda, J.L. (2011). Enhancing children's sport experiences and personal development: a motivational perspective. In R. Bailey & I. Stafford (eds), *Coaching children in sport* (pp. 123–138). London: Routledge.

Quested, E., Duda, J.L. & Appleton, P. (2011). A qualitative evaluation of coaches' implementation of the Empowering Coaching™ approach. *13th Annual Congress for Sport Psychology (FEPSAC)*, Madeira, Portugal, July 2011.

9

EXAMINING THE IMPACT OF THE FA YOUTH COACH EDUCATION PROGRAMME

Evidence of change?

Mark Griffiths, Kathleen Armour and Alexander De Lyon

Introduction

As we described in an earlier chapter, findings from research on traditional models of professional development suggest that many coaches perceive coach education as failing to meet their individual learning needs (Jones, 2006). For many, traditional approaches to continuing professional development (CPD) lack the relevance and context-specific knowledge to impact their practices. As a result, and where CPD is deemed irrelevant to a coach's individual needs, coaches may sometimes simply ignore new CPD material and continue with what they know, while giving the impression that they are taking new ideas on board (Chesterfield *et al.*, 2010). Indeed, what is striking from the relatively little research in the field of CPD for football coaches is a degree of consensus which suggests that existing CPD is divorced from the reality of practice (Jones & Wallace, 2005), does not take into account individual needs (Nelson & Cushion, 2006), is not sustained (Jones *et al.*, 2003) and uses evaluation procedures that allow for an attendance model of learning (Nelson *et al.*, 2013). Taken together, these findings mean that relatively little change has been captured in practice.

In response to this emerging research base, The Football Association (The FA) created The Football Association Youth Coach Education (FAYCE) programme in order to support coaches as learners *in situ*. The rationale of the programme was to deliver a personalised and needs-led professional development programme at the site of coaches' practice. The deployment of coach educators operating within the boundaries of the professional football club represented a unique opportunity to deliver contextualised professional knowledge. Underpinning the programme was an assumption that The FA had a role in supporting clubs and youth development, which in turn would improve selection, retention and training processes for talented young players. To achieve this, the FAYCE programme and its expansion set out to: increase the number of youth coaching awards taken in clubs; raise the profile of youth coaching and the learning function in clubs; and model and lead activity to promote more effective youth coaching. Building on these aims, the research set out in this chapter sought to examine the evidence of 'positive change' claimed by the programme in two areas: (1) coach learning within professional clubs; (2) promoting effective youth coaching practices. For the purpose of this chapter, positive change can be understood as the strengths, capabilities and possibilities of the programme.

Background

A review of the professional development literature suggests that change is in many ways a constantly occurring and inevitable part of practice. Yet, it is difficult to capture desired changes through new policy initiatives, as these will nearly always have unintended and/or unexpected consequences that lead to unpredictable results (Fink, 2003). Moreover, change will never take place in a simple linear or highly rational form; rather, it is a process that occurs in complex 'real-world' situations and environments, and is enacted by many different people. As a result, positive change is usually a gradual, inconsistent and challenging process which can take a considerable amount of time to occur. With this in mind, we drew on the concept of 'journey' or 'distance travelled' of participants in order to acknowledge participant development over time of the intervention, and the ways in which participants related to the intervention (Crabbe, 2006). Having previously worked with The FA on a pilot version of the programme, we were uniquely positioned to evaluate the 'distance travelled' by coaches and coach educators by comparing participant experiences between the pilot version of the programme and the rolled-out version of the programme described in this chapter.

During the initial phase of the research, we conducted a systematic search of existing research around organisational learning and change in the broad learning and educational literatures.[1] The search was conducted using computerised databases for all English-language research relevant to organisational learning/change published in academic journals between 2003 and 2013. The focus of the search was on evaluation/impact studies published in academic journal papers to learn from the current knowledge in these related fields. Table 9.1 provides information about the search protocols and terms used to review the literature, along with the returns from each database.

According to Guskey (2002), professional development programmes should be deliberate, purposeful endeavours with clear and well-defined objectives. This argument was supported by evidence obtained from a number of empirical studies retrieved from the literature search. For example, Bourke and McGee (2012) examined the processes and impact of a three-year cultural innovation which, they claim, created a visible change in an in-service teacher educator organisation in New Zealand. These authors suggested that successful individual and organisational changes were related to establishing a clearly recognised purpose, widening

TABLE 9.1 Initial database search for organisational learning, impact, evidence and change

	Organisational learning AND evidence		Organisational learning AND impact		Organisational learning AND change	
	Returns	Relevant, abstract read and available	Returns	Relevant, abstract read and available	Returns	Relevant, abstract read and available
ASSIA	121	13	121	12	608	21
ERIC	249	14	421	17	2,389	27
ProQuest – Education	288	16	489	21	2,917	28
Social Sciences Citation Index (ISI)	298	4	426	4	646	6
Zetoc	134	6	166	7	296	7

individual and group involvement and offering valued professional learning opportunities and resources that facilitated progress towards the overall goal.

Similarly, in a study exploring the impact of a nationally funded CPD programme aimed at 'transforming' standards of staff development in the United Kingdom (UK) further education system, Browne et al. (2008) showed that the nature of the objectives for a professional development programme and level of support are key factors influencing whether a programme is successful or not. Results of this study demonstrated how the restrictive nature of organisational support, combined with the widely ambitious, and at times idealistic, aspirations of the programme, were significant factors that limited its capacity for change. The study concluded that programme designers and policy-makers should make their intentions clear and engage with local programme managers on a regular basis. It was envisaged that such approaches are helpful for developing shared ambitions and allowing participants to actively change their practice which, in turn, acts to facilitate organisational transformation (Browne et al., 2008).

Results from the search showed there is a vast amount of literature related to organisational learning and change in the context of professional development programmes in education and elsewhere. This literature provides a useful body of evidence to demonstrate 'what works' in the implementation of new policy and/ or practice initiatives. However, it should be noted that despite the vast amount of literature in this area, results from the search suggested that there have been only a small number of relevant large-scale impact/evaluation studies conducted over the last ten years. Significantly, no studies were identified that attempted to evaluate the impact of professional development programmes on coaches' practices in football.

Summary of key points

- Existing research shows that organisational change is a complex, multi-layered/levelled and ongoing process, meaning that designing interventions that successfully achieve the intended positive changes can be notoriously difficult in practice contexts.
- In facilitating positive change, there is a need to consider the interaction between each of the different levels/layers of the organisation in relation to their broader organisational objectives.
- The effectiveness of any innovative intervention will depend upon the degree of coherence and communication between each of the different levels/layers, as well as the practices they help to shape.
- CPD interventions appear to be most effective at supporting positive change when they are deliberative, have realistic goals, and are based on clearly defined outcomes.
- There is a need to consider appropriate strategies to review, monitor and (collectively) evaluate innovative interventions.

FA case study research: key questions, methods and findings

The research questions

In seeking to identify the evidence of positive change claimed by the FAYCE programme, the following questions were addressed:

1. In what way do coach educators deliver individual learning activities to club coaches?
2. In what ways have club coaches used knowledge from individual learning activities and youth modules?
3. How does the FAYCE programme engage youth coaches in CPD?
4. What are the mechanisms of change claimed by the FAYCE programme that promote coach learning?

Two senior researchers and four research assistants at the University of Birmingham undertook research examining evidence of positive change from the FAYCE programme over a period of 12 months (March 2013 to March 2014).

Research methods

1. Focus groups with the coach educators.
2. Literature reviews: a systematic review of existing research into the concepts of impact and evaluation models was undertaken.
3. Interviews with key academy personnel, youth coaches and coach educators.

4. Data analysis: all interviews were transcribed verbatim, and field notes were written up immediately following site visits. Data were analysed independently by one senior researcher and two research assistants and themes were developed systematically from a synthesis of the two independent analyses.
5. Ethical clearance for the project was given by the University of Birmingham Ethics Committee. Respondents signed consent forms, and the researchers have taken steps to ensure individuals and clubs remain anonymous.
6. Sample: participant sample included: 10 coach educators, 13 academy managers/heads of coaching, 23 coaches (Premier clubs $n = 4$; Championship $n = 3$; League 1 $n = 3$; League 2 $n = 3$).

Research findings

RQ1: in what way do FAYCEs deliver individual learning activities to club coaches?

The distinctive value of the programme was the way FAYCEs delivered personalised learning activities for youth coaches. Grounded in the culture of the youth football academies, FAYCEs promoted learning activities that were authentic and relevant to the practices of the participating coaches engaged with youth modules. As a result, coaches (and academy managers) had begun to look at coaching in different ways as a consequence of the FAYCE programme, to deliver learning opportunities *in situ*. In this regard, the programme was led by the needs of the club. As two academy managers commented:

> We've taken all the training that The FA have given us and FAYCE's been brilliant. He's come in and said, 'Look, we can work with you individually, we can develop you that way.'
>
> *(Academy manager)*

> I think his role will vary depending on what club he's working with. You know, [FAYCE] has been really good because he's come in and said, 'Look, tell me what's working, tell me what you can – what we need to improve on?'
>
> *(Academy manager)*

It was interesting to note that there was consensus from academy managers and heads of coaching that younger coaches, in particular, would gain most from the programme. In contrast, there was acknowledgement that more experienced coaches might be more sceptical of another 'initiative':

> I think some of the older coaches it's just another thing, I think they can be a bit sceptical about, 'Oh, The FA are going to roll out another course and then in two years it means....' So when they hear things like, well once you get The FA Youth Award, all three modules, it's the equivalent of a UEFA

B, they go, 'Oh, will it be that in three years' time?' I think there's a bit of scepticism in there.

(Academy manager)

There was consensus from participants that the potential of the programme to influence coaches and promote change was an outcome of sustained contact with coach educators. The following quotes illustrate the importance of the interpersonal relationship between educator and coach in generating the learning experience:

> So I think what'll benefit will be coaches who would like somebody on a regular basis to give them feedback about what they're doing and what they see. That'll be a major contender.
>
> *(Academy manager)*

> In my view, young coaches would benefit from that longevity of relationship with their tutor, with The FA. It would justify the expenditure and the course costs. It would also take away this ludicrous area of being judged on a forty-minute exam or a twenty-minute assessment, as opposed to saying, 'Actually, let's watch this guy coach all year, X amount of times. Work with him, give him things to work on. Come back, monitor him again', which hopefully is the way that these coach educators are going. It's just on not a big enough scale, in my opinion.
>
> *(Academy manager)*

RQ2: in what ways have club coaches used knowledge from individual learning activities and youth modules?

Evidence suggested that FAYCEs had been successful in encouraging coaches to conceive youth coaching in new ways; namely by acknowledging the needs of individual learners and utilising language in such a way that fostered effective learning. Here, the coaches reported varied and innovative learning from the FAYCE engagement, which had then been taken forward into their coaching. There was an overwhelmingly positive response from coaches concerning the impact of the FAYCE programme on their coaching practices (e.g. content and delivery styles). In seeking evidence for coaches' use in practice of the information delivered through The FA youth modules, there was consensus that coaches were increasingly recognising the individual learner. For instance:

> A lot of our coaches haven't come from a teaching background if you like, so what's been good about the programme is it's made them think about the way that – well basically each player is individual and how to differentiate the groups.
>
> *(Head of coaching)*

What we've found is that the coaches have certainly bought into that as well. So they're now saying, 'Do you know, he's a fantastic player, but his attitude in training isn't great.' So we're now saying to them, 'Right, okay, so what little challenges, what little targets can you set?' Where before he may've not – he's got a bad attitude, right off he goes sort of thing and we can't take him because his attitude isn't right. Now coaches are thinking, well yeah, okay he's got a bad attitude but what can we do about it? I think it's made our coaches a lot more conscientious.

(Academy manager)

They would see new ways, and new methods and new ideas and new thoughts on how players should be developed, particularly younger ones.

(Academy manager)

RQ3: how does the FAYCE programme engage youth coaches in CPD?

Findings of the research demonstrated that the programme gave coaches access to new knowledge through the expertise of the coach educators. Specifically, one of the main strengths of the programme seemed to be that coaches were engaged in relevant problem identification/solving activities within a club setting. For the majority of coaches, the value of the FAYCE programme was access to sport-specific knowledge and wider pedagogical theory/practice.

It was interesting to note that both academy managers and youth coaches recognised the historical legacies from previous coach education experiences (for many a negative experience) and how the FAYCE was different because it created an environment for learning and development that was valued by the coaches/clubs:

A generation of coaches have come through that have been told what to do… and how to do it … coaches seem to be cloned. [FAYCE] has generated new ideas and encouraged coaches to deliver in their own style.

(Academy manager)

The process of upskilling coaches has been accelerated due to [FAYCE] involvement and the flexibility of him [FAYCE] coming here as opposed to us waiting for a course to be run that doesn't tie in with staff commitments. We're in a much better position than we were eight months ago.

(Academy manager)

I think it's made me more reflective on the sessions that I use, the language that I use to players, the things that we do. And I think the main thing I've taken away from it are values as a coach, it's made me think about what are my values, what are my beliefs, reflect and evaluate on what I'm doing. So I suppose it's trying to adopt that philosophy – because I know a lot of coaching you're told, 'Right. Stop. Stand still. I'll show you what went wrong.' But now it's: 'That's going right. Well done. Can you do more of that? Can you get better at...?' And if you've got all those tools in your locker, rather than just the hammer, you know, if you've got a screwdriver or something, I think I am trying to do things differently – so I think I'd be more reflective and looking at much more reflection in my actual practices.

(Youth coach)

A number of coaches reported changes in their coaching style and philosophies, often not dramatic changes but subtle adaptations:

I think I've changed. My style is more varied. I now work out when to be more command, and when to move to show and tell.

(Youth coach)

Another coach reported:

Definitely planning for me. It puts questions in the back of your mind, thinking is it relevant? Are they getting what they should be getting out of the practices? So, yeah, it has changed my way of coaching.

(Youth coach)

These points appear to echo findings of the wider learning and educational literatures, which show that professional development programmes are most effective at facilitating change when they target meaningful and gradual changes grounded in practice contexts, as opposed to trying to radically alter existing practices through off-site provision.

RQ4: what are the mechanisms of change claimed by the FAYCE programme that promote coach learning?

The mechanisms of change used by FAYCEs included (but were not limited to): critical reflection, introspection and mutual support. It is interesting to note the importance of the supporting role that coach educators played within each individual club. Described by coaches as 'useful to bounce ideas off', 'third-party support' and 'always available to have a chat about how things are going', the coach educators provided a sounding board for coaches outside of youth modules and practical assessments. The informal mentoring roles that coach educators played could, therefore, be regarded as one pivotal aspect for supporting positive change within football clubs.

Evidence suggested that there has been a significant cultural step change in the ways in which coach learning has been conceptualised in professional English football clubs. In this context, The FA was valued as a source of professional knowledge in facilitating positive change:

I think the most important thing is that the delivery of the modules has been the key. not just the module content itself, but the willingness to discuss, the willingness to challenge ideas; the willingness for the coaches to be able to have an opinion, where on other courses you're not encouraged to have an opinion, you're not encouraged to ask questions, it is, 'Our way or the highway'. And in this aspect of this FA programme, it's encouraging independent thinkers, it's encouraging change, it's encouraging that we don't know all the answers and you guys do it for a living and you might be able to add value to what we're doing, and vice versa.

(Academy manager)

For many academy managers, the value of FAYCEs was that it gave them access to the wealth of resources available at The FA. As one observed:

If we feel that we're short of an area, we need a bit more information; I'd say to [FAYCE], 'What do you know about this [FAYCE]? Could you tap into this anywhere within The FA system?' So I think from [FAYCE's] point of view and ours, I think it will be good for us.

(Academy manager)

Interestingly, a high number of academy managers suggested that in a crowded CPD space for coaches (e.g. also provided by the Premier League, League Managers Association, Football League), there was a need for The FA to establish an identity in promoting and supporting coach learning:

Interviewer: How do you see the role of The FA in terms of coach education?

Head of coaching: (Laughs) *It needs an identity. It's a very topical issue. Yeah, it needs an identity. It needs an identity massively. It works really well, because from an education point of view, and also but most important for me it's another set of eyes on the coaches.*

Implications

The aim of this chapter has been to examine the evidence of change claimed by the FAYCE programme in two areas (coach learning within professional clubs and promoting effective youth coaching practices). Specifically, the focus of the chapter has been to identify and explore factors that are associated with positive change, so that these factors can be optimised in innovative coach education programmes in the future. Taking all the evidence together, the following developments are supported by the data in this study.

Coach learning within professional football clubs

The value of a coach education intervention such as the FAYCE is that it is grounded in the needs of the club. However, the successful development and implementation of a 'needs-led CPD' is arguably dependent on the way in which 'need' is interpreted, analysed and assessed.

The programme offers a personalised learning experience, and is a good example of a needs-led approach to coach learning. The programme was highly valued for delivering coach education in-house. The FAYCE programme has facilitated a shift in the way youth coaching is conceived and delivered. Coach learning occurred in three areas: thinking, practice and self-confidence.

Promoting effective youth coaching practices

Positive change was a consequence of sustained contact between the FAYCE and club coaches. The FAYCE programme has promoted improved communications between youth football academies and The FA. Moreover, evidence from the study suggests that coach educators in the programme are increasingly taking up informal mentoring roles within clubs and they will need support helping youth coaches develop their cognitive skills in progressing towards an increasingly autonomous/expert position.

As we have reported in a previous chapter ('CPD provision for the football coaching workforce'), the lack of systematic evaluation systems that enabled coach educators to obtain extensive feedback from both coaches and players (as the ultimate end-users) was identified as a major missing link in the current system. There is therefore a need to consider programme evaluation methodology in two areas:

1. Develop a model that is context-sensitive to the social, cultural and political dimensions of football youth academies.
2. Establish baseline measurements as early as possible to better understand the impact of CPD programmes.

The majority of coaches and academy managers in this study valued the FAYCE programme for its flexibility in delivering coach learning opportunities *in situ*. In this regard, the FAYCE programme offered The FA an opportunity to establish a credible presence for quality coach development within clubs. However, in realising the potential of the programme, there is a need to consider the interactions between different levels/layers of The FA organisation in relation to their broader learning objectives. Coaches and academy managers, for example, described how different layers of The FA, historically, have advocated different coaching philosophies. As we concluded in our review of the organisational change literature, the effectiveness of any policy intervention will depend upon the degree of coherence and communication between each of the different levels/layers and the practices they help to shape.

Within the context of The FA's coaching youth modules, it is clear that the FAYCE programme objectives included developing and providing coaches with opportunities to engage with (new) ideas and principles. It is important, however, for the programme to consider its role in supporting coach learning beyond the youth modules, focusing on, for example, innovation, problem-solving and creative thinking to achieve effective changes in coaches' practices. In this regard, coach educators in the programme will themselves need professional development support in constructing teaching and learning strategies that facilitate and support youth coaches' ongoing learning.

We have also noted in this research the importance of identifying clear learning theories in the design and structure of coach development aspirations. This becomes even more important as The FA seeks to develop robust evaluation frameworks. More work is needed on the learning approaches (e.g. Adult Learning Theory) that underpin the design of different learning initiatives, their consistency in application and the ways in which anticipated outcomes are congruent with those theories. Therefore, the findings of this research suggest that in order to achieve their learning goals, sports organisations might find it helpful to consider the following:

1. What are the learning and support needs of coach educators?
2. What learning theories/approaches underpin the design and structure of any learning programme?
3. How will organisations develop evaluation models that are context-sensitive to the social, cultural and political dimensions of sport?
4. How will organisations ensure a degree of coherence and communication between each of the different levels/layers of the organisation that are charged with coach education?

Note

1   It should be noted that due to the dearth of football CPD literature, the databases selected for the searches and overall search strategy were focused on retrieving studies from the broader learning and educational literatures.

References

Bourke, R. & McGee, A. (2012). The challenge of change: using activity theory to understand a cultural innovation. *Journal of Educational Change*, 13, 217–233.

Browne, L., Kelly, J. & Sargent, D. (2008). Change or transformation? A critique of a nationally funded programme of continuous professional development for the further education system. *Journal of Further and Higher Education*, 32 (4), 427–439.

Chesterfield, G., Potrac, P. & Jones, R. (2010). 'Studentship' and 'impression management' in an advanced soccer coach education award. *Sport, Education and Society*, 15 (3), 299–314.

Crabbe, T. (2006). *'Going the Distance': impact, journeys and distance travelled: Third Interim National Positive Futures Case Study Research Report*. London: Home Office.

Fink, D. (2003). The law of unintended concequences: the 'real' cost of top-down reform. *Journal of Educational Change*, 4, 105–128.

Guskey, T.R. (2002). Professional development and teacher change. *Teachers and Teaching*, 8 (3), 381–391.

Jones, R.L. (2006). The sports coach as educator: reconceptualising sports coaching. *International Journal of Sports Science and Coaching*, 1(4), 405–412.

Jones, R.L. & Wallace, M. (2005). Another bad day at the training ground: coping with ambiguity in the coaching context. *Sport, Education and Society*, 10 (1), 119–134.

Jones, R.L., Armour, K.M. & Potrac, P. (2003). Constructing expert knowledge: a case study of a top-level professional soccer coach. *Sport, Education and Society*, 8 (2), 213–229.

Nelson, L.J. & Cushion, C.J. (2006). Reflection in coach education: the case of the national governing body coaching certificate. *Sport Psychologist*, 20 (2), 174.

Nelson, L., Cushion, C. & Potrac, P. (2013). Enhancing the provision of coach education: the recommendations of UK coaching practitioners. *Physical Education and Sport Pedagogy*, 18 (2), 204–218.

10

PRACTICE ACTIVITIES DURING COACHING SESSIONS IN ELITE YOUTH FOOTBALL AND THEIR EFFECT ON SKILL ACQUISITION

Paul R. Ford and Jordan Whelan

Introduction

The development of youth players into expert professional players is a key concern of clubs, governing bodies, coaches and support staff. Players engage in multiple coaching sessions across their youth that are aimed at developing the skill and knowledge required for expert performance in the professional game. The aim of this chapter is to review previous research and theory on the practice activities that football players engage in during coaching sessions. Two new research studies are presented that examine practice activities in elite youth football coaching sessions, as well as knowledge and skill acquisition in both coaches and players.

Practice or training activities in football should lead to skill acquisition in players that transfers to retained improved performance in match-play. The practice activities used during coaching sessions can be split into two categories that have different effects on skill acquisition in players. *Drill-based activities* are those in which the coach pre-determines the decisions for players so that they are not actively making them when engaging in the practice. Drill-based activities include fitness training, technique practices and some skills practices in which players are not active decision-makers. *Game-based activities* are those in which players are actively making decisions themselves based on the positioning of teammates, opponents and space. These activities include small-sided games, unidirectional games, possession games, phases of play and some skills practices in which players are active decision-makers in the same manner as during match-play. Games-based activities are predicted to lead to greater improvements in the ability of players to use vision to scan and make decisions during match-play, when compared to drill-based activities (Ford, in press; Ford & Williams, 2013; Ford *et al.*, 2010; Low *et al.*, 2013).

Researchers have investigated the proportion of youth coaching session time spent in drill-based versus games-based activities. The practice activities occurring in 70 coaching sessions led by 25 coaches of child and adolescent teams from the elite, sub-elite and recreational level in England were examined by Ford *et al.* (2010). Coaches had their players engage in drill-based activity for 65 per cent of session time and games-based activity for 35 per cent of session time, with few differences reported across skill or age groups. Similarly, Low *et al.* (2013) investigated the coaching sessions of child and adolescent cricket players at recreational and elite level in England. Players spent 69 per cent of session time in drill-based activity and 19 per cent in games-based, with the remaining percentage of time spent in transition between the two activities, again with very few differences across skill or age groups. These findings (Ford *et al.*, 2010; Low *et al.*, 2013) show that youth athletes often engage in high amounts of drill-based activity during coaching sessions, which is likely limiting acquired skill transfer to match-play.

Some researchers have investigated why coaches use the practice activities they have players engage in. Partington and Cushion (2013) interviewed 11 coaches of elite youth football players in England about why they use their practice activities. Coaches stated that they used drill-based activities due to a lack of pitch space in which to use games-based activities. They further stated they used their practice activities to develop decision-making in players. No researchers have examined the sources from which coaches first acquire the practice activities they use during their sessions. However, other researchers (Erickson *et al.*, 2008; Wright *et al.*, 2007) have investigated the sources of general coaching knowledge of coaches in Canada. They interviewed 35 volunteer youth ice hockey coaches (Wright *et al.*, 2007) and 44 coaches of various sports working across age groups (Erickson *et al.*, 2008) about the sources of their coaching knowledge. In both studies, coaches stated their knowledge was acquired from playing and coaching the sport, from coach education, from printed and electronic material, and by observing and interacting with other coaches, including formal mentors. These studies (Erickson *et al.*, 2008; Wright *et al.*, 2007) show that coaches acquire both craft and professional knowledge. Professional knowledge is based on relatively certain scientific evidence and theories, and is often disseminated through coach education. Craft knowledge is described as 'knowing-in-action' as it is the practical knowledge that guides the various steps and actions of the performance itself.

Formal coach education is a key process from which coaches acquire the various aspects of their performance. In 2010, The Football Association (The FA) launched *The Future Game* guide in which one aim is 'to produce technically excellent and innovative players with exceptional decision making skills' (The FA, 2010: 5). In recent times, they have launched coaching courses with content designed to achieve this aim, such as The FA Advanced Youth Award and The FA Youth Award Modules. In part, these courses are thought to advocate that coaches increase the number of games-based activities used in their coaching sessions. Ideally, content delivered on coaching courses leads to relatively permanent change(s) in coach behaviour that, subsequently, leads to greater skill acquisition in players (Ford *et al.*, 2009). Therefore, coach education course content that advocates increasing the number of games-based activities used in practice sessions should lead to coaches who participated in the course using more of this activity in their sessions. The increase in games-based activity used by these coaches should improve the ability of their players to use vision to scan the match-play environment and to make decisions.

FA case studies research: key concepts

In the following section, two new research studies are reported that examine the types of practice activities used by coaches of elite youth football players in England, as well as knowledge and skill acquisition in both coaches and players.

Study 1

The aim of this study was to examine the practice activities used by coaches of elite youth players in England. The idea was to investigate whether the amount of games-based activity had increased in 2013 following the implementation by The FA of new coach education courses, when compared to the data reported by Ford *et al.* (2010). A further aim was to examine why coaches use the activities they have players engage in and where they first acquired them. It was expected that the amount of games-based activity used by coaches would have increased when compared to the Ford *et al.* (2010) data, probably due to modern coach education courses. Coaches are expected to have acquired the activities from both craft and professional knowledge sources (e.g. Wright *et al.*, 2007) and to use them to develop skills in players, such as decision-making (e.g. Partington & Cushion, 2013).

Three elite English clubs took part in the study, consisting of two child teams (9–11 years of age) and two adolescent teams (14–16 years of age) and their coaches from each club's youth academy. The two age categories (child, adolescent) were chosen because athlete age is a contextual factor that requires differences in coach performance and knowledge (Côté *et al.*, 2007). Expert coaches of child athletes (aged 5–11 years) are expected to provide opportunities for athletes to engage in fun and enjoyable low-organisation games-based activities. In contrast, expert coaches of skilled late adolescent athletes (aged 15–18 years) are expected to provide opportunities for athletes to engage in deliberate practice activities seeking to improve sport-specific and fitness attributes (Côté *et al.*, 2007). For each of the 12 teams, three in-season coaching sessions were filmed, making a total of 36 sessions across teams and clubs.

The video footage of the coaching sessions was analysed for the proportion of time spent in drill- and games-based activities. Drill-based activity is that in which the coach pre-determines decisions for the players so that they are not actively making them when engaging in the practice. These activities include fitness training, technique practices and some skills practices. Games-based activities are those in which players are actively making decisions themselves based on the positioning of teammates, opponents and space. These games include small-sided games, unidirectional games, some skills practices, possession games and phases of play. The proportion of session time spent in transition between these two activities was analysed and mean session duration calculated.

Following the block of coaching sessions, we interviewed the 12 coaches of the teams about their reasons for using the activities and their acquisition sources. For the interviews, six activities were chosen from the three sessions of each coach, ensuring a somewhat equal spread across the six different sub-activity types (fitness activity, technique practice, skills practice, small-sided games, possession games, phase of play). In the interviews, for each practice activity, coaches were shown the activity and asked the questions: (Q1) 'What were your reasons for using this activity?' and (Q2) 'Where did you first acquire that activity from?'. Interviews included probes and prompts when necessary. Interview responses were used to create categories containing the frequency of reasons cited per activity and the frequency of acquisition sources.

Findings

The average duration of the 18 sessions for the child teams at the three clubs was 93 minutes (SD = 14). Figure 10.1a shows the proportion of drill-based activity, games-based activity and transitions between activities during these coaching sessions. The coaching sessions for the child teams contained 63 per cent (SD = 12) of games-based activity, 20 per cent (SD = 13) of drill-based activity and 17 per cent (SD = 5) of transition between activities. The mean duration of the 18 sessions for the adolescent teams at the three participating clubs was 90 minutes (SD = 13). Figure 10.1b shows the proportion of games-based activity, drill-based activity and transitions between activities during these coaching sessions. The coaching sessions across the adolescent teams contained 56 per cent (SD = 14) of games-based activity, 21 per cent (SD = 14) of drill-based activity and 23 per cent (SD = 7) of transition between activities. These findings show a significant increase in the proportion of games-based activity during elite youth coaching sessions compared with that found by Ford *et al.* (2010; 40 per cent of games-based activity for elite teams).

Since there were few differences between the practice activities of the coaches working with child and adolescent players, the interview responses were combined to include those from all 12 coaches. Coaches cited their main reasons for using games-based activity as developing tactical knowledge (23 responses; 24.5 per cent), developing technical skill (18 responses; 19.1 per cent), developing decision-making (14 responses; 14.9 per cent), the academy curriculum (14 responses; 14.9 per cent) and making the activity game realistic (12 responses; 12.8 per cent). These responses were more frequent compared to improving fitness (4 responses; 4.2 per cent), other (6 responses; 6.4 per cent) and the activity being age appropriate (3 responses; 3.2 per cent). Coaches cited their main reasons for using drill-based activity as for preparation for the session (17 responses; 40.5 per cent) and

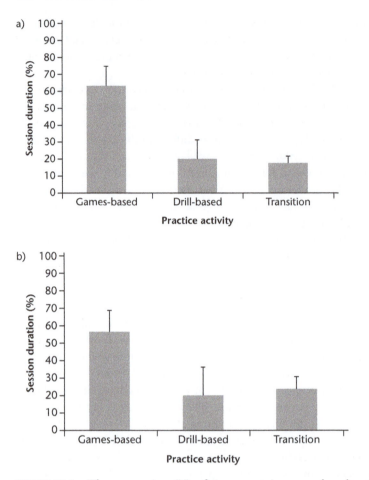

FIGURE 10.1 The proportion (%) of time spent in games-based activity, drill-based activity, and transition between activities during the coaching sessions of (a) the child teams and (b) the adolescent teams.

developing technical skill (10 responses; 23.8 per cent). These responses were more frequent compared to the academy curriculum (6 responses; 14.2 per cent), age appropriateness (2 responses; 4.8 per cent), a progression before game-play (2 responses: 4.8 per cent) and other (5 responses; 11.9 per cent). The coaches cited their main acquisition source for the activities as other coaches (23 responses; 47.9 per cent). Other acquisition sources were coach education courses (9 responses; 8.8 per cent), created on their own (7 responses; 14.6 per cent), coaching books (3 responses; 6.3 per cent) and a mix of other coaches and a coach education course (5 responses; 0.4 per cent).

Study 1 findings show that the amount of games-based activity in the sessions led by coaches of elite youth players in England has increased in 2013 compared to that detailed in the Ford *et al.* (2010) study. In the Ford *et al.* (2010) study the amount of games-based activity for the elite teams across age groups was 40 per cent of session time. In the current study, in 2013, the amount of games-based activity across age groups was 60 per cent of session time. The increase in games-based activity is probably due to modern coach education interventions that advocate a greater use of this activity in youth coaching sessions. However, coaches tended to first acquire the activities through craft knowledge sources, such as observing other coaches, to a greater degree than professional knowledge sources. It is likely that coaches acquired professional knowledge regarding the importance of decision-making from coach education, which they used to select the activities they observed from other coaches and we examine this idea further in Study 2. They demonstrated awareness as to why they used their activities, such as using games-based activity to develop decision-making, albeit with some contradictions, such as stating they used drill-based activities to develop decision-making.

Study 2

The aim of this study was to examine the effectiveness of a coach education course in changing coach behaviour and, subsequently, player skill acquisition. We expect the coaching course to advocate and, subsequently, to lead to an increased amount of games-based activity in practice sessions occurring after the course compared to before it. The resultant increase in games-based activity should be associated with an increased amount of visual scanning by players during small-sided games after the course and sessions compared to before it.

Participants were three coaches of elite players aged 10–11 years from three separate English youth academies. The coaches successfully participated in The FA Advanced Youth Award. Prior to the course, three coaching sessions from each of the three coaches were video recorded, making a total of nine sessions. Video footage was analysed for the amount of time spent in games- and drill-based activity. Moreover, after the three coaching sessions, the coaches' players took part in an 8 vs. 8 game that was filmed. Game footage was analysed for the frequency of visual search and scanning conducted by the players during the game. The frequency of head turns was used as a proxy for the amount of visual scanning. After the small-sided games, the coaches took part in The FA Advanced Youth Award course (AYA). During the course, the coach educators were interviewed about the main goals of the content on the course. Moreover, a content analysis was conducted on the AYA course resources that were provided to the coaches during the course, which included the course booklet and the Future Game DVD and USB for coaches of players aged 8–11 years. These resources were analysed to determine the types and frequencies of practice activities within them, as well as to assess the amount of information on the topics of practice structure, decision making and visual scanning. Immediately following the course, the coaches and their players took part in the same procedure as before the course in which three sessions and one game were filmed and analysed. At the end of the study, the coaches were interviewed in an attempt to reveal what they had learnt from the course and to provide rationales for their coach behaviour after their participation in the course. There were 17 players who participated in both small-sided games before and after the course. Players who took part in only one game were removed from the analysis.

Findings

Figure 10.2 shows the proportion of coaching session time spent in games-based activity, drill-based activity and transitions between activities before and after the course. Before the course, the mean duration of the sessions was 85 minutes (SD = 10). Those sessions contained 49 per cent (SD = 8) of games-based activity, 30 per cent (SD = 7) of drill-based activity and 21 per cent (SD = 5) of transition between activities. After the course, the mean duration of the sessions was 76 minutes (SD = 15). Those sessions contained 67 per cent (SD = 9) of games-based activity, 11 per cent (SD = 9) of drill-based activity and 22 per cent (SD = 9) of transition between activities. Data show more games-based activity in the sessions after the course (67 per cent, SD = 9) when compared to before it (49 per cent, SD = 8). Moreover, there was less drill-based activity in the sessions after the course (11 per cent, SD = 9) when compared to before it (30 per cent, SD = 7). The coaches' main reasons for increasing the amount of games-based activity was the influence of their participation on The FA AYA, as well as to develop decision-making, to make their training sessions more game-realistic, and external reasons, such as the club curriculum.

Before the course, the mean duration of the small-sided games was 21 minutes (SD = 4). Those small-sided games contained an average of 106 head turns per

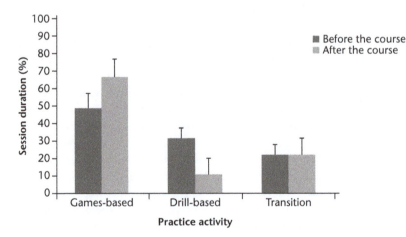

FIGURE 10.2   The proportion (%) of time spent in games-based activity, drill-based activity and transition between activities during the coaching sessions of the youth teams at the three clubs before and after the coach education course.

player (SD = 28), equating to 5.1 head turns per minute. After the course, the mean duration of the small-sided games was 19 minutes (SD = 6). Those small-sided games contained an average of 118 head turns (SD = 29), equating to 6.6 head turns per minute. The amount of visual scanning was greater after the course and sessions (6.6 head turns per minute, SD = 1.5) when compared to before them (5.1 head turns per minute, SD = 1.6).

Three of the AYA coach educators were interviewed in an attempt to understand the information on the course. The interview focused on course content related to: (1) games- and drill-based activities; (2) practice design or structure; and (3) visual scanning or search and decision-making. The coach educators stated that content on these topics was regularly provided through the formats of the course booklet, coaching practicals, lectures or workshops from specialist external speakers in this area, a secure online website containing the presentations and video practicals, visits by the coach educators to the clubs, and through general discussion and group work. The general consensus of all three coach educators during the interview was that a key aim of the AYA course was to provide information to increase the amount of games-based compared to drill-based activity and to increase knowledge about improving decision-making in youth players.

Table 10.1 shows the type and frequency of information on these topics within the AYA course booklet. The importance of decision-making and practice structure in youth football was highlighted on multiple occasions in the booklet. It highlighted the importance of using games-based activities on numerous occasions and contained 15 examples of these practice activities. There was one example activity in the booklet that was categorised as a drill-based. The Future Game DVD and USB for coaches of players aged 8–11 years contained 37 examples of games-based activities and five examples of drill-based activities.

Study 2 findings show that the amount of games-based activity used by the three coaches of elite youth players in their sessions significantly increased by 18 per cent following their participation in The FA's AYA course. The coaches cited their participation in the course as a main reason for their increased their use of games-based activity. The players of these coaches demonstrated a greater amount of visual scanning during small-sided games after the course and sessions compared to before it. The course itself and its resources provided the coaches with information aimed at increasing the amount of games-based activity used in coaching sessions, as well as the ability of players to use vision to scan the match-play environment and make decisions. However, there are some limitations in this study that suggest caution when interpreting its findings. First, the increase in the visual scanning of the players following the course may simply be associated with and caused by engagement in the sport across time, rather than the increase in games-based activity following the course. Second, although the coaches stated the course led to the observed increase in games-based activity following it, some other factors may have led to the increase, such as natural variation in the activities used across time.

TABLE 10.1 The type and frequency of information on practice activities and decision-making provided within the Advanced Youth Award course booklet

Information	Frequency	Example quote
Designing practice and structure	19	'The design of the practice should challenge players to "scan", "assess" and "anticipate" the movement of the ball, team-mates and the opposition. Monitoring the game in this way will help players improve their sense of awareness and understanding of space and time, which in turn will improve their decision making and technical execution.'
Importance of decision–making	11	'Developing game understanding and decision-making should be encouraged in this age group. Players should be given lots of opportunity to take part in game-related practice, with coaches challenging players to solve problems within small-sided games.'
Importance of practice structure	2	'Most expert football players are products of a life-long dedication to self-improvement, accumulating thousands of hours of practising and playing games along the way.'
Contradictory practice structure	1	'Some players will need more constant practices.'
Total	*33*	

Implications

The implications of these studies are that modern coach education that advocates greater use of games-based activity, such as The FA Youth Award Modules, appears to have led to the desired change in coach behaviour. In Study 1, the coaches used greater amounts of games-based compared to drill-based activity. In Study 2, a course that advocated the increased use of games-based activities in coaching sessions led to that outcome and the transfer of skill in players from these activities to improved match-play performance. However, further work is required because the activities analysed did not fully correspond to the principles derived from research. On average, 30–40 per cent of session time consisted of drill-based activity from which transfer of skill to match-play is compromised, as well as transitions between activities. Moreover, some of the games-based activities analysed did not contain key evidence-based principles of practice derived from research (for a review, see Ford, in press; Ford & Williams, 2013). First, many of the games-based activities lacked *specificity* because players were making movements, actions and decisions that looked and were different to those they normally make during match-play (e.g. many activities occurred on astro turf in very small areas of play). Second, there did not appear to be a systematic approach by the coaches to ensure players experienced repetition of attempts at *all* of the key skills, situations, contexts and tactics that form the game and that are required for expert performance to develop.

The implications emanating from the interviews are that coaches must fully understand the reasons for using the activities they have players engage in so that they can ensure those activities are optimal for skill acquisition. Coach education can play a role in ensuring coaches better understand why they use the practice activities they have players engage in by disseminating evidence-based information on practice structure, visual scanning and decision-making. Moreover, coaches need to become reflective practitioners so that they can integrate craft knowledge into their practice (e.g. when observing an activity being used by another coach) where it aligns with professional knowledge (e.g. a better understanding of why they use the activities), and vice versa. To some degree, the coaches in these studies may have been integrating knowledge sources in this way because they chose to use activities acquired from observing other coaches that conformed to professional knowledge being disseminated on coach education courses (i.e. increased use of games-based activity and the importance of decision-making). However, reflective practice is a well-developed area of professional knowledge (e.g. Knowles *et al.*, 2014) and coach education can play a central role in disseminating this information and creating coaches who are reflective practitioners. A better understanding of why coaches use the activities will allow them to critically reflect on the quality of the activities they use to ensure those activities are optimal for skill acquisition in the sport (Cushion *et al.*, 2012).

There is a need for coach educators, coaches and researchers to work more closely together in order to ensure coaching and education processes are evidence-based and optimised. Researchers are constantly conducting and publishing new research that could inform and optimise coaching practice and education. Therefore, coach education courses must be *research-informed* so that they can consistently update their content with this new evidence when it becomes available, rather than waiting until the course is revalidated some time later. A few coach education courses already do this to some degree by inviting researchers to present their work on the course. Furthermore, researchers must ensure that they conduct, publish and present research that answers key applied questions from coaches and coach educators. In the area of practice and instruction, for example, further research is required on the best instruction and feedback strategies for skilled individuals and to develop tactical knowledge. In addition, the studies reported in this chapter were short in duration and further work is required to examine whether the observed changes are permanent.

Summary

In this chapter, previous research and theory on the practice activities that youth players engage in during coaching sessions were reviewed. Games-based activities should lead to greater improvements in the ability of players to use vision to scan and to make decisions during match-play when compared to drill-based activities. Therefore, coaches of youth players should seek to use games-based activities in all of their many varieties during their sessions to a greater extent compared to drill-based activities. Two new research studies were presented that examined practice activities in elite youth football coaching sessions, as well as knowledge and skill acquisition in both coaches and players. Findings showed that coaches of elite youth players were using greater amounts of games-based compared to drill-based activity in their sessions and that the amount increased after a coach education intervention. However, the coaches mainly acquired these activities from observing other coaches, suggesting they used the professional knowledge acquired from coach education about the importance of decision-making in players to guide their decisions on which activities to use.

Critical questions

When observing, creating or leading any practice activities in coaching sessions there are four critical questions that can be used to assess their effect on skill acquisition:

1. In the activity, are the players actively making decisions in the manner they would normally do during match-play based on the positioning and movements of teammates and opponents, and space?
2. In the activity, are the players making movements, actions and decisions that look and are the same as those they make during match-play (e.g. actions executed, distances, situations)?
3. Does the practice activity suit the age and skill level of the players who will engage in it or who are engaging in it? Is it too difficult or too easy for those players and, if so, how can it be adapted to meet a level of challenge suitable for their current status?
4. The amount of practice is positively related to attained performance level, so practice time should be optimised. Therefore, during the session, is the duration of the transition between activities too long and how can it be reduced?

References

Côté, J., Young, B., North, J. & Duffy, P. (2007). Towards a definition of excellence in sports coaching. *International Journal of Coaching Science*, 1, 3–17.

Cushion, C., Ford, P.R. & Williams, A.M. (2012). Coach behaviours and practice structures in youth soccer: Implications for talent development. *Journal of Sports Sciences*, 30, 1631–1641

Erickson, K., Bruner, M.W., MacDonald, D.J. & Côté, J. (2008). Gaining insight into actual and preferred sources of coaching knowledge. *International Journal of Sports Science & Coaching*, 3, 527–538.

Football Association, The (2010). *The future game: The Football Association technical guide for young player development.* London: FA Learning.

Ford, P.R. (in press). Skill acquisition through practice and other developmental activities. In T. Strudwick (ed.), *Soccer science*. Champaign, IL: Human Kinetics.

Ford, P.R., Coughlan, F. & Williams, A.M. (2009). The Expert Performance Approach as a framework for understanding and enhancing coaching performance, expertise and learning. *International Journal of Sports Science & Coaching*, 4, 451–463.

Ford, P.R. & Williams, A.M. (2013). The acquisition of skill and expertise: the role of practice and other activities. In A.M. Williams (ed.), *Science and soccer III* (pp. 122–138). London: Routledge.

Ford, P.R., Yates, I. & Williams, A.M. (2010). An analysis of practice activities and instructional behaviours used by youth football coaches during practice: exploring the link between science and application. *Journal of Sports Sciences*, 28, 483–495.

Knowles, Z., Gilbourne, D., Cropley, B. & Dugdill, L. (2014). *Reflective practice in the sport and exercise sciences: contemporary issues*. London: Routledge.

Low, J., Williams, A.M., McRobert, A.P. & Ford, P.R. (2013). The microstructure of practice activities engaged in by elite and recreational youth cricket players in England. *Journal of Sports Sciences*, 31, 1242–1250.

Partington, M. & Cushion, C.J. (2013). An investigation of the practice activities and coaching behaviours of professional top-level youth football coaches. *Scandinavian Journal of Medicine and Science in Sport*, 23, 374–382.

Wright, T., Trudel, P. & Culver, D. (2007). Learning how to coach: the different learning situations reported by youth ice hockey coaches. *Physical Education and Sport Pedagogy*, 12, 127–144.

11

COACHING DISABLED FOOTBALLERS

A study of the coach journey

Annette Stride, Hayley Fitzgerald and Ellie May

Introduction: setting the scene for disability football coaching in England

Like many national governing bodies (NGBs) of sport, The Football Association (The FA) is committed to coach development. At the heart of coach development is a desire to create reflective practitioners who embrace life-long learning to promote meaningful experiences for those they coach (Lyle & Cushion, 2010). Through its coach education programme, The FA signposts a commitment to its broader goal of 'football for everyone' (The FA, 2011) and a responsibility to work towards inclusion and anti-discrimination (The FA, 2015). For example, a range of opportunities are offered to support coaches to better understand how to work with disabled footballers. In part, the impetus for targeting disabled footballers comes from a broader recognition that this group has a 'right' to sport (United Nations, 2006). Indeed, The FA and other NGBs have engaged in activities to raise levels of participation and performance in sport among disabled people. These activities include supporting coach development, and this chapter considers The FA's Coaching Disabled Footballers (CDF) course. To offer a wider context to this course, the chapter begins with a brief literature review that considers disabled sport and the concept of inclusion. After this, selected findings are presented from a larger CDF research project. Specifically, consideration is given to CDF course participants' motives, aspirations and satisfaction with the course. The chapter concludes by exploring the implications of this research for The FA, NGBs and researchers.

Disability, sport and football

The following literature review focuses on disability sport and disability football, specifically considering: (a) participation by disabled people, (b) coaching disabled people and (c) sports volunteers and coaches with disabilities.

Participation by disabled people

Over the past 15 years there has been a steady increase in research projects focusing upon disabled people's participation in, experiences of and attitudes towards sport (Rankin, 2012; Simeonsson *et al.*, 2001; Sport England, 2002). The findings from this research reflect a number of inequalities in participation. For example, disabled adults participate less in sport, particularly those with an 'ambulation' disability, and women and Asian people with disabilities. Research also demonstrates that disabled people have a reduced breadth of experiences within sport than non-disabled adults. For example, disabled people are under-represented in sports volunteering, coaching, club membership and NGB representation. Encouragingly, the most recent Active People Survey shows football as the fourth most popular sport played once per week by disabled people (English Federation of Disability Sport, 2013). Other research has explored disabled people's experiences of playing football, (Macbeth & Magee, 2006; Stride & Fitzgerald, 2011) and spectating (de Haan *et al.*, 2013; Paramio-Salciness & Kitchin, 2013).

Coaching disabled people

Limited research has been undertaken focusing on the learning, development or expertise of coaches working with disabled people in sport (Young, 2010). The small-scale research undertaken suggests coaches' biographies influence their initial and ongoing commitment to coaching disabled people. Moreover, offering multiple and diverse learning opportunities was found to better support coaches working with disabled people (McMaster *et al.*, 2012). Research undertaken from the perspective of disabled athletes produces some interesting findings. First, athletes are aware that some coaches lack confidence and can be reluctant to coach disabled athletes. Second, disabled athletes believe coaches need a combination of sports-specific technical knowledge and a good understanding of their athletes to effectively support them. Third, disabled athletes value opportunities to share their knowledge about themselves with their coaches (Fitzgerald, 2013).

Sports volunteers and disabled coaches

A common limitation of studies on disabled people who volunteer within sport is that disabled people are often grouped into the category 'people at risk of social exclusion' (that also includes members from Black and minority ethnic communities and the unemployed). However, the 'Helping Out' study (Low *et al.*, 2007) does consider people at risk of social exclusion and disabled people separately and found an under-representation of disabled volunteers within sport. Additionally, a national study (Sport England, 2006) found that disabled people volunteer in sport at lower levels than non-disabled people. Data available from Sports Coach UK indicates that the majority of community sports coaches (CSCs) in the UK are male (70 per cent), British White (92 per cent) and non-disabled (98 per cent) (Townend & North, 2007). According to North (2006), disabled coaches are less likely to access coach development opportunities such as coaching conferences and mentoring.

This brief review demonstrates that there remains a need for focused research exploring the participation, experiences and attitudes of disabled athletes (including footballers) and coaches. This chapter reports on a study exploring the experiences of those involved in organising, delivering and participating in The FA's CDF course, specifically addressing:

1.   What are the experiences of coaches attending CDF courses (focusing on expectations, knowledge and skills gained, attitudes and anticipated and actual usefulness)?
2.   What are the aspirations of coaches in relation to coaching disabled footballers?
3.   What are the key factors and circumstances that support coaches' aspirations?
4.   How do coaches apply the CDF course content in their coaching practice?
5.   Is the CDF course fit for purpose in its current form?

As it is beyond the scope of this chapter to review all of the findings from this research, two are focused upon here that contribute to addressing the research questions: (1) CDF participants engaging with course content; and (2) CDF course strengths and areas for development. Before providing the findings, the key concepts of the case study research are discussed, including the Inclusion Spectrum as an integral part of the CDF course, and the methodology underpinning the study.

The FA case study research: key concepts

The Inclusion Spectrum

The Inclusion Spectrum (Figure 11.1) is an activity-based model that has been adopted internationally by many governing bodies of sport and disability sport organisations. Through five delivery approaches it can contribute to the inclusion of *all* participants, including those with disabilities, in sports and physical activity sessions.

In an 'open' activity, all participants do the same activity together without modification of the activity. This increases levels of participation for the whole group and helps to build participants' confidence. In 'modified' skills, participants continue to work together, sharing their strengths and abilities. While everyone does the same task there are changes to rules, areas or equipment for some individuals. In 'parallel' games, the same type of activity is undertaken by everyone.

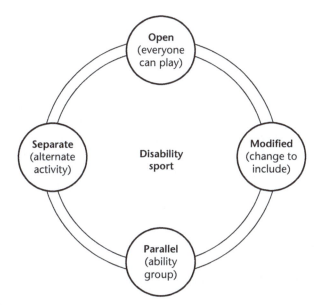

FIGURE 11.1 The Inclusion Spectrum (© Stevenson and Black, adapted from Stevenson, 2009).

However, different groups participate in different ways and at different levels. As young people develop skills they can change groups. 'Separate' activities involve participants engaging separately, either as individuals or as a team. A separate activity allows extra coaching to occur which may build confidence and skills to enable participation with the main group. In 'disability sport' non-disabled participants take part in an activity that has a disability sport focus, often called 'reverse integration' (Stevenson, 2009). The extent to which the Inclusion Spectrum is adopted by CDF coaches is discussed later in the findings.

Methodology

The research adopted a multi-method approach to data collection, including the following. (a) A questionnaire distributed to approximately 4,800 past CDF course participants with 408 completed. (b) An international benchmarking exercise with the four Home Nation FAs, three international FAs and three wider sport organisations. This recorded information on disability coach education including course features, participant profiles and course content. (c) Case studies of five county FAs where 25 interviews were completed with county FA officers, CDF tutors and CDF course participants. (d) A web presence audit of the five county FA websites exploring the online presence and visibility of disability football provision. (e) Attendance at two CDF courses to gain more in-depth insights, achieved by (1) one researcher participating in the course, (2) another researcher acting as a roving reporter, gathering sound bites from course participants and (3) creating a secure Facebook group to provide a source of support for course participants and a means of collecting additional data from participants post-course.

In analysing these data, the online system used to host the questionnaire enabled the generation of a series of descriptive statistics which the researchers analysed for recurring patterns and trends. Qualitative data (interviews, Facebook posts and field notes from CDF course attendance) were analysed in stages. First, following the constant comparison method the qualitative data were read and re-read before being coded (Lincoln & Guba, 1985). Second, interview data were cross-referenced back and forth to other data with memos used to articulate links between the different sources. Third, the use of detailed notes and memos led to the development of more refined themes and sub-themes. The research gained ethical approval from Leeds Beckett University Research Ethics Committee.

Research findings

The CDF participants engaging with course content

Data from the questionnaires revealed the majority of CDF participants are male (82 per cent), 'White British' or 'White English' (85 per cent) and non-disabled, a profile similar to that of other coaching courses. Encouragingly, 12 per cent of CDF participants self-identified as experiencing a disability, a higher proportion than other governing body courses (Townend & North, 2007). Participants had a range of experiences, with 58 per cent coaching players with disabilities. When participants were asked what had motivated them to attend the CDF course, or what their aspirations were in taking part in the course, seven key responses were evident from the questionnaire and interview data. Table 11.1 provides an overview of these motives.

The main motive concerned increasing knowledge and understanding of coaching disabled people. In this regard, there was a concern that specific expertise around coaching disabled people was not adequately addressed in other coach development opportunities undertaken.

It is widely recognised within coach development research that participating in formal coach education may not necessarily lead to any changes to practice (Cassidy & Jones, 2008). It is encouraging to note that 84 per cent of CDF participants indicated that they had drawn upon some aspects of the course content in non-disabled football coaching contexts. Table 11.2 summarises participant responses concerning specific aspects of the CDF course content that are used in both disability football and non-disabled football coaching.

Course content focusing on adapted practices, communication and learning styles were used most in disability football and non-disabled football contexts. However, according to the questionnaire responses, more theoretically oriented content focusing on long-term player development, the Inclusion Spectrum and STEP seems to be used to a lesser extent. Interestingly, the interviews revealed that particular aspects of the Inclusion Spectrum were often drawn upon when coaching.

TABLE 11.1 Motives for attending the CDF course

Motive	Illustrative questionnaire responses
1 Increase, enhance or improve knowledge and understanding of coaching people with disabilities	'I did the CDF course to get more knowledge of players who have disabilities. This was excellent for my players as they got better training sessions as I had more knowledge after doing this course. Before the course I didn't know how to adapt sessions to players' abilities and after the course it really helped.'
2 To gain more insight into coaching practices, skills and techniques when working with players with disabilities	'I had been coaching disabled players for over a year and I wanted to develop my skills to ensure I was giving the best sessions possible to my disabled players.'
3 Wanting to work in a disability sport setting	'After I completed my Level 1 I got to see all the different pathways and I wanted to coach disability football as I don't think the kids and adults get a chance to play in mainstream football.' 'It is something I am interested in. I currently coach my own children, my son is now 16 so I won't be coaching him for much longer. I've had years of coaching junior football and I thought it would be good to broaden my horizons.'
4 Useful for current role (e.g. schools, colleges, community work and sports clubs)	'I was implementing a pan-ability for all college students and was looking to gain a greater understanding of the range of disabilities I could encounter and how to ensure my session engages all.'
5 Requirement (e.g. of current job or part of CPD hours)	'As a club disability coach it was a requirement.' 'My CPD for licensed coach.'
6 To enable them and their club to offer a more inclusive environment for all abilities	'I believe in inclusion and if there is a way to involve everyone in sport I will do what I can to be able to facilitate that; and in taking the CDF course it enabled me to do just that.'
7 Personal reasons (e.g. disabled themselves, disabled family members or encounters with disabled people leaving them feeling ill-equipped)	'My son has Cerebral Palsy (CP) and I wanted to help out at his CP football club. I also wanted to see if there were any technical practices and games I could adapt and modify when coaching mainstream players, while also including him in the coaching sessions.'

TABLE 11.2 Using CDF course content in disability football and non-disabled football

CDF course content	Disability football (%)	Non-disabled football (%)
Adapting practices	67	67
Coaching players with specific impairments	50	29
Long-term player development	23	36
Inclusion Spectrum	35	32
STEP (space, task, equipment, people)	34	37
Player pathways	21	21
Competition structure	17	15
Health and safety	37	37
Terminology	43	40
Communication	56	59
Learning styles	49	55
Not used any of the course content in this context	19	16

> Like parallel games, you don't need disabled kids. In any group you have skill rich kids and skill poor kids. If there's anything that course should do its influence getting parallel games into standard coaching.
>
> *(CDF participant)*

> It really helped me in Powerchair. We've got some kids who are extremely poor in skills and ability and some incredibly rich. Some kids are in their chairs, all over the place, it's like watching wasps, and at this end you've got some kids who don't move much faster than snails but they're really in the same group. Having been on the course they do exactly the same thing within what they can but the argument is always aspire to get to the next group.
>
> *(CDF participant)*

> The first session we did after the CDF was our best session ever. Without a shadow of a doubt, parallel games, lots of changes, lots of movement, looking at different people's abilities. We just came away, I was like, that was brill.
>
> *(CDF participant)*

What the interviews reveal is that CDF participants are utilising aspects of the Inclusion Spectrum but are not necessarily recognising the model as a whole. It seems that CDF participants have been able to distinguish which aspects of the model are more or less applicable within their coaching settings.

CDF course strengths and areas for development

In relation to CDF course reflections, all data sources indicated a number of areas with high levels of satisfaction, illustrated in Table 11.3.

The qualitative comments identified by different participants also expressed considerable satisfaction. For example, course participants highlighted how they valued the tutors' knowledge and approach, the combination of practical and theory, the course's relevance, cost, and the opportunity to share experiences and concerns with other coaches. FA tutors and officers added to this, suggesting the course was good at dispelling myths, alleviating coaches' fears and being a good introduction to working with disabled footballers.

While there were more comments emphasising what works well in relation to the course, some dissatisfaction was highlighted, including the lack of post-course support, course length, and course content. In relation to lack of post-course support, various stakeholders suggested that more guidance was needed regarding how to get involved in coaching disability football, information about other courses and contact information for teams and relevant local groups. The following comments are typical of those made.

> Progression is an issue. You complete the CDF course but then what is the next step? Where do I go next? I want to know more but once you had finished the course that was it, no more communication about what to do next, no development or progression?
>
> *(CDF participant)*

> I feel what is important is that post-course participants need to get experience and the development officer should facilitate contact with clubs to ensure that they can get that experience.
>
> *(CDF tutor)*

TABLE 11.3 Course satisfaction

Aspect of satisfaction	Percentage 'satisfied' or 'very satisfied'
Pre-course information	95
Suitability of the venue	97
Relevance of course content	96
Time spent in the classroom	96
Time spent doing practical	91
Tutor's approach and delivery	99
Cost	99

The end of the course is rushed, after the practical. For me, the player pathway should be local to your area, you have got this or that going on. Even just a leaflet from The FA officer would be good.

(CDF tutor)

Regarding course length, participants commented on the amount of content covered in one day. Participants identified key areas that could be extended to increase course duration, including: practical content; insights into identifying/ classifying some disabilities; more theoretical engagement; and information about specific impairments.

There is so much to cover around disability that one day isn't enough. There was nowhere near enough time to do any decent practical and gain feedback.

(CDF participant)

The idea of including coaching people with disabilities, and in particular people with different impairments, in the practical aspect of the course generated much discussion. Indeed, it was felt this addition would enable theory to be put into practice.

No delivery with disabled players was a massive negative. So was not enough time to talk about specific impairments.

(CDF participant)

The course needs to be more practically based and would be enhanced with people with impairments being part of the course for the practical sessions.

(CDF tutor)

Other ways in which disabled people could take a more active role in the CDF course were also discussed, including the opportunity to observe the coaching of disabled players at elite and recreational level, and listening to disabled players talking about their footballing experiences and challenges encountered. Others mentioned having the coaching of disabled footballers as a requirement post-course.

The length of the course should be increased to include a couple of days' course content, followed by a break to try out course content, and then to return for another session, and then on the last day coach a team of disabled adults/children.

(CDF participant)

In relation to course content, various stakeholders identified the need for more in-depth understandings of specific impairment groups.

The course particularly lacks how to deal with learning disabilities.

(FA officer)

There are many groups that have come to the fore since the course was written. I'm talking here about mental health issues and Aspergers. These are issues that the coaches seem to come across more and more in mainstream situations.

(CDF tutor)

In summary, the findings from this research suggest the CDF course has a number of key strengths and areas for potential development. The CDF course participants, FA tutors and officers all offer valuable insights about the course that have implications for The FA, NGBs and researchers.

Implications for The FA

One of the key implications of this research for The FA is to consider the extent to which the CDF course continues in its current form or is changed in order to extend the nature and scope of disability-related courses offered by The FA. To some extent, both of these developments could build on the limitations discussed earlier. In terms of the current CDF course, no respondents suggested the removal of any of the course content. However, there were a range of suggestions made about adding content but clearly this would need to be considered in relation to extending the length of the course.

If the CDF course was extended, a number of potential areas were recommended, such as impairment-specific content (learning disability, behavioural and mental health issues), and including disabled people as football participants. Additionally, course participants expressed a desire to continue their development after the CDF course and suggested improvements to post-course support. These included the development of a simple leaflet outlining clubs and volunteering opportunities, and a database of contacts (e.g. clubs, opportunities and volunteers). Further signposting for follow-up courses and initiating an information exchange for sharing good practice, offering support and Q&A forums were also seen as important. The Facebook dimension of this research demonstrated that some CDF participants value the opportunity to engage interactively. Therefore, the possibilities of using social media as a means of communicating with CDF participants post-course could be explored.

Any extension of the CDF course in terms of increasing the content and therefore the length would have wider implications in relation to how it fits within the current framework of FA accredited courses. A number of potential opportunities were expressed by different respondents, including developing a course which has formal credit (e.g. CDF Level 1 and 2), integrating the CDF content into existing provision (e.g. FA Level 1 or Youth Modules) and extending the current range of impairment-specific courses. The development of courses with formal credit would bring The FA in line with a number of other governing bodies featured in the benchmarking exercise.

Implications for NGBs

A number of areas of good practice were evident within the case study county FAs. While the findings evidencing this good practice are not reported in this chapter, it is worth briefly reviewing this good practice as this could inform wider NGB work supporting coach development aimed at enhancing disabled people's experiences.

1. In a number of county FAs, officers appear to have developed strong partnerships within their county. Their ability to effectively network is key to developing these partnerships. Other NGBs should consider how they can promote inter-county or regional partnerships.
2. A number of county FAs supported regular meetings with course tutors (of different courses offered in the county). This enabled non-CDF tutors to better understand the course and promote it to participants of different courses. Other NGBs should consider how they can promote regular county or regional tutor discussions to improve tutors' knowledge and maximise the range of course options publicised to course participants.
3. A number of county FAs had systems in place capturing information about coaches and volunteers within the county. This enabled CDF courses to target specific groups and individuals. Other NGBs should consider the extent to which their processes enable this tracking of coaches and volunteers and put in place a system that supports bespoke targeting of additional coach development opportunities.

Implications for researchers

To ensure the original research questions for this project were answered, and indeed, to fulfil The FA's requirements, the research tools used to gather data were carefully considered. It was recognised that quantitative methods are an ideal way of reaching large audiences relatively easily and quickly. Such methods can capture precise, numerical data regarding attitudes and behaviour or organisational practice (Neuman, 2014; Punch, 2014). Thus, a benchmarking exercise and a questionnaire to past CDF participants were employed. It was also acknowledged that a short, online survey could reach the majority of past course participants, generating data that could be generalised across the entire population. Although surveys and benchmarking tools are useful in establishing answers to simplistic questions, they are less likely to provide detailed answers regarding participants' motives and aspirations. In this regard, qualitative methods such as interviews were ideal in establishing the experiences and thoughts of different stakeholders involved in the organisation, delivery and participation of the CDF course (Sparkes, 2002).

The researchers also acknowledged that alternative methods are increasingly employed in sports research to break down barriers between the researcher and the researched while providing different means of communicating to suit individual needs (O'Sullivan & MacPhail, 2010). Thus, attendance at courses and the use of the secure Facebook group were also drawn upon. In using a diverse range of methods, data analysis and representation becomes increasingly complex. This chapter presents only a snapshot of the data generated and in the final report the researchers used a series of critical non-fictional narratives. Narratives, or stories, are often employed as a means of weaving together disparate data sources and presenting them in a coherent way. The researchers also recognised that the accessibility of stories can enable practitioners, policy-makers and planners in sport to make better sense of the data than if more abstract data had been presented.

Critical questions

1. Is it better to have separate coach development in relation to including disabled people in sport? An alternative could be to infuse understandings of disability into all coach development. Identify a specific sport and consider which of these approaches would be most suitable and why.
2. Should the coaching system promote sport-specific disability coaches or should all coaches have some knowledge and expertise in coaching disabled people?
3. To what extent should disabled people feature in coach development as tutors, coaches or athletes for coaches to work with? What are the implications of such involvement?
4. In this chapter the key focus has been upon coach development through a short course. What other kinds of multiple and diverse learning opportunities could be developed to promote a more holistic approach to a coach's journey?

References

Cassidy, T.G. & Jones, R. (2008). *Understanding sports coaching: the social, cultural and pedagogical foundations of coaching practice*. London: Routledge.

de Haan, D., Faull, A. & Kohe, G.Z. (2013). Celebrating the social in soccer: Spectators' experiences of the forgotten (Blind) Football World Cup. *Soccer and Society*, 15, 578–595.

English Federation of Disability Sport. (2013). *Sport England active people survey 7: participation in individual sports*. Loughborough: English Federation of Disability Sport.

Fitzgerald, H. (2013). *Disabled Performers' Reflections of Sports Coaching*. Leeds: Sports Coach UK.

Football Association, The. (2011). *The FA group strategic plan 2011–2015*. London: The FA.

Football Assocation, The. (2015). *English football's inclusion and anti-discrimination action plan season 2013–2014 update and focus for the future*. London: The FA.

Lincoln, Y.S. & Guba, E.G. (1985). *Naturalistic inquiry*. Beverley Hills, CA: Sage.

Low, N., Butt, S., Paine, A.E. & Davis Smith, J. (2007). *Helping out: a national survey of volunteering and charitable giving*. London: The Cabinet Office.

Lyle, J. & Cushion, C. (eds) (2010). *Sports coaching: professionalisation and practice*. London: Elsevier Ltd.

Macbeth, J. & Magee, J. (2006). 'Captain England? Maybe one day I will': career paths of elite partially sighted footballers. *Sport in Society*, 9, 444–462.

McMaster, S., Culver, D. & Werthner, P. (2012). Coaches of athletes with a physical disability: a look at their learning experiences. *Qualitative Research in Sport, Exercise and Health*, 4, 226-243.

Neuman, W.L. (2014). *Social research methods: qualitative and quantitative approaches*. Harlow: Pearson.

North, J. (2006). *Community sports coach profile survey report*. Leeds: Sports Coach UK.

O'Sullivan, M. & MacPhail, A. (eds) (2010). *Young people's voices in physical education and youth sport*. London: Routledge.

Paramio-Salciness, J.L. & Kitchin, P.J. (2013). Institutional perspectives on the implementation of disability legislation and services for spectators with disabilities in European professional football. *Sport Management Review*, 16, 337–348.

Punch, K. (2014). *Introduction to social research: quantitative and qualitative approaches*. Thousand Oaks, CA: Sage.

Rankin, M. (2012). *Understanding the barriers to participation in sport*. Loughborough: English Federation of Disability Sport.

Simeonsson, R.J., Carlson, D., Huntington, G.S., Sturtz McMillen, J. & Lytle Brent, J. (2001). Students with disabilities: a national survey of participation in school activities. *Disability and Rehabilitation*, 3, 49–63.

Sparkes, A. (2002). *Telling tales in sport and physical activity: a qualitative journey*. Leeds: Human Kinetics.

Sport England. (2002). *Adults with a disability and sport national survey 2000–2001*. London: Sport England.

Sport England. (2006). *Active people survey headline results*. London: Sport England.

Stevenson, P. (2009). The pedagogy of inclusive youth sport: working towards real solutions. In H. Fitzgerald (ed.), *Disability and youth sport*. London: Routledge.

Stride, A. & Fitzgerald, H. (2011). Girls with learning disabilities and football on the brain. *Soccer and Society*, 12, 457–470.

Townend, R. & North, J. (2007). *Sports coaching in the UK II*. Leeds: Sports Coach UK.

United Nations (2006). *Convention of the Rights of Persons with Disabilities*.

Young, J. (2010). The state of play: coaching persons with disabilities. *Coaching and Sport Science Review*, 50, 9–10.

12

THE PROGRESSION OF BLACK AND MINORITY ETHNIC FOOTBALLERS INTO COACHING IN PROFESSIONAL FOOTBALL

A case study analysis of the COACH bursary programme

Steven Bradbury

Introduction

This chapter will begin by drawing on recent research evidence which has highlighted the low levels of Black and Minority Ethnic (BME) representation as coaches in professional football and identified a range of key constraining factors that have limited the progression of BME groups across the transition from playing to coaching in the professional game. The chapter will then offer some case study analysis of the COACH bursary programme, a positive action initiative designed to offer support to 150 BME coaches to achieve high-level coaching qualifications and undertake placement opportunities at professional clubs. In doing so, the analysis will draw on evaluation of the first year of the COACH bursary programme to identify and examine some of the beneficial impacts incurred by participants and participating clubs. The chapter will then conclude by offering some wider analysis as to the extent and ways in which the COACH bursary programme has challenged and disrupted some ongoing racialised inequalities in the sport, as well as drawing attention to some key organisational shortcomings of the programme to this end. Finally, this concluding section will discuss the potential implications of these findings for the promotion and delivery of improved equality and diversity practices within professional football and across other sporting contexts.

State of knowledge and literature review

Over the past 60 years the UK has steadily become one of the most ethnically and culturally diverse countries in Europe. As of 2014, around 14 per cent of the 63 million strong population of the UK is drawn from BME backgrounds, the majority of which is resident in England. However, the extent to which the 'super-diversity' of

English society is fully represented within the various tiers of professional football remains partial and mixed. For example, while around 25–30 per cent of all adult and youth players at professional clubs are drawn from BME backgrounds, this cohort is primarily made-up of 'Black' and 'Mixed Ethnicity' players. In contrast, the number of players from South Asian backgrounds at professional clubs remains markedly low (Burdsey, 2007). Further, despite the longstanding involvement of (some) BME players in the professional game, there has thus far been only a limited transition from playing into coaching positions in the sport among these groups (Bradbury, 2014). Similarly, the demographic make-up of the senior administrative and governance tiers of professional football remains almost exclusively White (Bradbury, 2013; Bradbury et al., 2011, 2014). To this end, these variable patterns of BME representation support Back et al.'s assertion that the 'assimilation of "black" people within the national imagination as sports heroes need not in any way be congruent with access to the centres of decision making and institutional power' (Back et al., 2001: 5).

Recent research has examined in some detail the levels of representation of BME coaches in professional football in relation to coach education qualifications and coach employment (Bradbury et al., 2014; Bradbury, 2014; 2015). In the first instance, this research has reported on the generally low numbers and progressive drop-off rate of BME coaches achieving qualifications across each stage of the 'core' coach education pathway in England. For example, it indicates that in July 2014, while 8.2 per cent and 7.4 per cent of FA UEFA B and FA UEFA A awards were held by BME coaches, just 6.9 per cent of FA Pro-Licence holders were from BME backgrounds. In the second instance, the research has reported that, in September 2014, only 19 out of 552 senior coaching positions at 92 professional clubs in England were held by BME coaches: 3.4 per cent of all positions of this kind. It also indicates that these overall percentage figures remain fairly constant when broken down across senior coaching categories at clubs and that they compare unfavourably with levels of BME representation as players (25–30 per cent) and in the UK population more broadly (14 per cent).

This recent research has also sought to 'give voice' to the first-hand experiences of elite-level BME coaches and other key stakeholders in English football to identify and explain the reasons for the low levels of BME coaches achieving coach education qualifications and accessing senior coaching positions at professional clubs. To this end, it has outlined a number of constraining factors which have limited the pace of BME progression across the transition from playing to coaching the game. These constraining factors include:

1. Limited access to and negative experiences of the high-level coach education environment. Findings here allude to limited opportunities for identification, selection, mentoring and financial support, perceived favouritism shown towards White peers, and experiences of intentional and unintentional racism at clubs and coach education courses. This is felt to have limited the aspirations and engagement of BME coaches in the coach education process and positioned them at a competitive disadvantage in the professional football coaching market place.

2. The continued over-reliance on networks- (rather than qualifications-) based methods of coach recruitment at professional clubs, premised on processes of personal recommendation, patronage and sponsored mobility. Findings here suggest these 'racially closed' methods of coach recruitment tend to favour White coaches drawn from within dominant social and cultural 'insider' networks. This is felt to be evidenced in the frequency with which, often less qualified, White coaches regularly access paid coaching positions at different clubs.

3. The continued existence of conscious and unconscious racial bias and stereotyping in the coaching workplace. Findings here refer to misplaced cultural perceptions with regard to the aspirations, attitudes, behaviours and intellectual capacities of BME coaches, and questioning the suitability, authority and competence of BME coaches to successfully coach and manage at professional clubs. This is felt to have led key decision-makers at clubs to view BME coaches in terms of (mis)perceived ethnic and cultural traits rather than in terms of their qualifications, experience and abilities as coaches and to have come to negatively conceptualise the appointment of BME coaches with 'uncertainty' and 'risk'.

4. Finally, the research has referred to the relationship between experiences of discrimination referred to above, the historical lack of BME coach role models and the cumulative impact of this in maintaining the low levels of BME coaches in the sport. In particular, this is felt to have acted as a key disincentivising factor in limiting the aspirations, ambitions and motivations of BME former players to undertake coach education qualifications and pursue coaching careers in the English professional game.

The research concludes that, taken together, the conscious and unconscious processes and practices of racial exclusion identified above constitute a form of institutional discrimination, and that this has thus far limited the realisation of equality of opportunities and outcomes for BME coaches in the professional game. In doing so, the research suggests that any measures or initiatives designed to address this ongoing racialised imbalance must remain cognisant of the relationship between under-representation and institutional discrimination and should seek to challenge and disrupt the structures which underpin this unequal state of affairs. It is to an analysis of one such initiative, the COACH bursary programme, that this chapter now turns.

FA case study research: the COACH bursary programme

About the COACH bursary programme

The COACH bursary programme is a positive action initiative funded by The FA which aims to provide practical and financial support to 150 BME coaches over a three-year period from 2012 to 2015. The central aim of the programme is to help BME coaches to achieve relevant coaching awards and undertake year-long placement opportunities at selected professional football club youth academies. To this end, the programme has been designed to address some racialised barriers to progression for aspiring coaches from BME backgrounds and to increase the levels of representation of BME qualified coaches working within the professional game. The COACH bursary programme is managed by Brendon Batson on behalf of The FA, with input from The FA's wider equality team. The programme also has whole-game support and includes advisory input from the Premier League, the Football League, the Professional Footballers' Association, and the League Managers Association.

The findings in this chapter are drawn from an evaluation of the first year of the COACH bursary programme conducted by the author (Bradbury, 2014b). During this initial period, the programme supported 45 BME coaches to undertake coaching qualifications and established placement opportunities at 25 professional clubs. The evaluation involved conducting an online survey of all first-year bursary coaches and semi-structured interviews with a further ten bursary coaches and six club mentors involved in placement activities at six case study clubs. This mixed-methods approach yielded a range of useful quantitative and qualitative data and allowed the research team to explore the 'journeys' of bursary coaches and placement clubs across their involvement in the programme. Key areas of investigation included: participants' demographic, educational and employment background and their prior qualifications and experiences of coaching; participants' programme-based coach education and club placement activities and experiences; the effectiveness of processes of mentoring and support at club placements; and the impact of the programme in engendering a series of beneficial outcomes for participants and placement clubs. It is an analysis of these beneficial outcomes to which we now turn.

Some key benefits for participants

Survey- and interview-based evaluation of the COACH bursary programme indicated a range of beneficial outcomes for participants at the individual, interactional and aspirational level. For example, at the individual level, more than three-quarters (78 per cent) of bursary coaches indicated that undertaking coach education courses and club placements had led to increased personal and professional development skills. To this end, bursary coaches noted improved self-esteem, confidence and communication skills and an increased knowledge and understanding of key technical and practical aspects of delivering coaching to elite-level young players in professional club academy environments. Central to factors underpinning these developmental benefits was the mutually reinforcing relationship between the pedagogical advances enabled by youth-oriented coach education courses and the experiential learning engendered by 'hands-on' participation in club placement activities. This was felt by bursary coaches and club mentors to have engendered a positive arc of personal and professional development for bursary coaches over the duration of their involvement with the COACH programme. The interviewees below comment further on these benefits and the processes through which they were incurred:

> The courses I have attended have changed my approach to football coaching and encouraged me to reflect on my coaching style. I believe I now have the confidence to coach anywhere and I'm more aware of aspects that could affect my coaching in the coaching environment.
>
> *(Coach survey respondent 13)*

> While I was on the placement I felt that I was advancing. In every session I was learning something new. I was pretty well qualified, to UEFA B level, but I don't think the UEFA B gets you prepared for working with that type of [younger] age group at all. So between the youth modules and the placement, it did advance me as a coach definitely.
>
> *(Coach interviewee 1)*

At the interactional level, around four-fifths (82 per cent) of bursary coaches reported that coach education courses and club placements had enabled increased opportunities to network with and learn from other coaches. To this end, bursary coaches and club mentors referred to the benefits of internal networking at communal coaching sessions and in-service training events, and external networking at weekend match-day and competition events involving other clubs. This was felt to have enabled opportunities for bursary coaches to observe highly qualified and experienced youth academy coaches, to better understand the processes of delivering age-related coaching practices and drills, and to establish clear templates of quality criteria against which to inform and measure progress. They were also felt to have helped to broaden the contact-base of bursary coaches and to heighten their visibility, status and credibility within professional club coaching networks. For example:

> Sometimes the real benefit of a course is the interactions with other coaches as well as with the educators. It was ideal to chat and compare ideas and concepts used during the session and draw upon their experiences.
>
> *(Coach survey respondent 25)*

> I think that [the bursary coach] has learnt a great deal about the delivery of the various topics that we've got on our programme from observing others and the opportunity to talk to people about the content. He's taken opportunities to come in and watch other coaches work with the older age groups. So from observing others he's learnt about the content, about the delivery of it, and about the philosophy of the club.
>
> *(Club mentor interviewee 2)*

Around four-fifths (82 per cent) of bursary coaches also referred to beneficial outcomes in terms of increasing aspirations towards undertaking further coach education courses and pursuing careers as coaches in professional football. To this end, bursary coaches and club mentors alluded to the experiential impact of the programme in encouraging reflections as to the social and professional suitability and competence of bursary coaches to work with specific age cohorts of elite-level young players. This process of reflection was felt to have reshaped the initial career preferences of some bursary coaches and to have led to a more targeted approach to undertaking relevant (largely youth-oriented) coach education qualifications. Further, bursary coaches and club mentors noted the impact of the programme in expanding initially limited aspirations of bursary coaches and establishing much stronger ambitions to access permanent part-time and full-time coaching positions at professional clubs. The interviewees below comment further on the shifting aspirations and enhanced employability of bursary coaches in this respect:

> I think when I came into it, I was thinking of working with the older groups, you know, the 15s, 16s, up to development squad level. But I picked up so much from doing the youth modules and I started to think that maybe I was better suited to working with the younger age groups, you know, at the foundation level. Sort of making sense of and applying what I was learning through the youth modules, and putting it into practice with the younger age groups.
>
> *(Coach interviewee 5)*

> I feel my aspirations have changed and increased, the more time I spent at the club. I want to do my B Licence over the next year and to have a full-time role within a professional club academy. I feel really optimistic and confident that this might happen now. I'm much more employable now. I don't think that would have happened if I hadn't been based at [the placement club] and I hadn't had the experience that I've had.
>
> *(Coach interviewee 8)*

Some key benefits for clubs

Survey- and interview-based evaluation of the COACH bursary programme indicated a range of beneficial outcomes for participating clubs. For example, in the first instance, club mentors alluded to the positive impact of accessing suitably qualified bursary coaches at little or no cost. This was felt to have helped support the organisational expansion of professional club youth academies as part of their commitment to meet the requirements of the new Elite Player Performance Plan (EPPP). A number of club mentors also alluded to the tendency of bursary coaches to be drawn from a range of different educational and employment backgrounds to existing coaching staff. This was considered to enrich the diversity of the social and professional skill sets of the youth academy workforce at clubs and to enhance the potential to provide a better overall service to client groups of young academy players. The influx of new, often young, bursary coaches was also felt by some club mentors to have helped to realise some key organisational intentions with regard to providing a fresh outlook and approach to the technical and social 'feel' of coaching at youth academies. Finally, club mentors alluded positively to the largely voluntary efforts of bursary coaches and their willingness to make extended unpaid coaching contributions within youth academy contexts. This was considered to provide a strong indicator of the ambition, diligence, work ethic and personal commitment of bursary coaches to pursue careers in the professional game as coaches and to enhance their employability to this end.

A number of interviewees also referenced the positive impact of the COACH programme in increasing the levels of BME representation at professional clubs. This was felt to have complemented wider efforts to better reflect the ethnic diversity of young players at youth academies and the multi-ethnic residential locales in which many placement clubs were geographically situated. A number of bursary coaches and club mentors expanded further on the qualitative impacts of these statistical advances in BME coach representation. In the first instance, these interviewees alluded positively to the potential and realised abilities of bursary coaches to 'connect with' and offer greater cultural awareness and understanding of the wider social experiences of young BME players. Related, a number of club mentors commented on the positive 'knock on' effect of establishing a more racially diverse coaching workforce at youth academies, with particular respect to better developing their own understanding of ethnic and cultural difference and improved approaches to 'diversity management'. Taken together, the addition of bursary coaches was felt to have increased the range of 'cultural options' for young BME players (and their families) to build relationships with coaching staff and to have enabled a more welcoming, inclusive and supportive environment to this end. Second, a number of bursary coaches and club mentors also referred to the key added value component of involvement in the COACH bursary programme in terms of the capacity of bursary coaches to act as positive role models to young BME players. This was cited in relation to supporting the playing advancement of young BME players and in terms of raising awareness among young BME players as to opportunities to pursue pathways as qualified coaches in the professional game for those who may otherwise drop out of the academy system. The interviewees below comment further on these positive impacts:

> Having the bursary coaches at the club is important. Having ethnic minority coaches is important. I think players of an ethnic minority background are then potentially going to be made to feel more comfortable having a fellow coach that's of an ethnic minority background, because I think that might be something that's important. It might not bother a player at all, but at least you know that it's something that has a potential to have a positive effect rather no effect at all, or, worst case, some sort of negative effect.
>
> *(Club mentor 6)*

The two guys, they're black guys, so it allows the club to be able to learn culturally. So me myself, I'm a white member of staff, so I'm able to speak to them and find out any experiences that they've got from their background. Obviously our club has lots of different players with all different types of culture and background so it helps the club to be able to have coaches who can relate to players and that type of thing. If there's ever issues that maybe we don't understand, then it's always worth getting different opinions isn't it from that point of view.

(Club mentor interviewee 4)

You've got to be honest, a lot of the players in this city they're from Black African, Black Caribbean backgrounds. So for them to see other ethnic coaches instead of the normal sort of middle-class white coaches, it gives them some kind of comfort at times to know that, you know, 'whatever I choose to do if I'm not a player, if I want to be a coach then I can go and do it, if they can do it we can too'. It's just letting them see that, you know, no matter what colour skin you have you can do it.

(Coach interviewee 2)

Implications of findings for key stakeholders

The findings presented in the previous section offer a useful starting point for further analysis as to the extent and ways in which the COACH bursary programme has challenged and disrupted some ongoing racialised inequalities in the sport. In particular, those structurally and culturally embedded processes and practices of institutional discrimination identified in the opening section of this chapter which have thus far constrained the progression of BME groups across the transition from playing to coaching in the professional game. To this end, we might argue here that the COACH bursary programme has had some partial success on this score. For example, in the first instance, the programme has helped to circumvent some key barriers to accessing coach education in relation to the identification, selection and provision of financial support for bursary coaches to undertake courses of this kind. Further, the positive experiences and development impacts engendered through these pedagogical encounters has had an identifiable knock-on effect in increasing (rather than decreasing) motivations and aspirations towards further qualifications of this kind among bursary coaches. Second, in enabling opportunities to access year-long club placements, the programme has enabled significant numbers of bursary coaches to break into – and gain the first steps on the ladder within – some historically closed professional club coaching networks. This is especially important given the findings of recent research which alludes to the ongoing 'catch 22' situation faced by many BME coaches who report lacking sufficient practical experiences of coaching elite level players to be considered for posts at professional clubs, while simultaneously being denied opportunities to gain experiences of this kind at clubs. Third, and related, the findings in the previous section indicate that the consistency of involvement in club placement activities has allowed bursary coaches opportunities to further develop and showcase their social and technical abilities and skill sets and prove their competence to senior coaching staff at clubs. In doing so, it can be argued that the COACH bursary programme has provided a mechanism through which to challenge prior misplaced perceptions on the part of key decision-makers at clubs with respect to the aspirations, attitudes and abilities of BME coaches to make a positive contribution to the club coaching environment. Fourth, and finally, the COACH bursary programme has arguably had the positive effect of establishing a small but significant core of identifiable BME coach role models at placement clubs. It is the contention here that this process might conceivably have wider ramifications in increasing the motivations of aspiring BME coaches within or outside of the COACH programme as to the realisable possibilities of pursuing careers as coaches in the professional game.

Beyond the more positive assertions above, it is, however, important to locate any analysis of the wider impact of the COACH bursary programme within its relatively limited scope and context. To this end, it is important to note that the programme represents a relatively small-scale attempt to increase the involvement of BME coaches in the professional game. For example, the programme has primarily focused its attention towards placing bursary coaches within the professional club youth academy environment. Further, it features no contractual obligation on the part of clubs to offer regular employment to bursary coaches at the end of their year-long 'unpaid internship'. While this arguably represents a pragmatic and manageable approach to the delivery of this 'resource limited' programme, it does also call into question the permanency of the developmental benefits incurred by bursary coaches and the likelihood of them accessing meaningful paid employment as coaches at professional clubs. As a result, it can be argued that it is unlikely that the COACH programme in its present guise has or will have any dramatic impact in increasing the overall percentage levels of BME coaches in the professional game, at least in the short to medium term. Further, where some limited statistical gains do become present, they are likely in the first instance to be at youth academy level rather than in terms of senior coaching positions at professional clubs.

It is important here also to highlight some key structural and organisational shortcomings of the management and delivery of the first year of the COACH programme. To this end, survey- and interview-based data alluded to a series of factors which were felt to have limited the potential of bursary coaches and participating clubs to fully engage with – and help to realise the aims and objectives of – the COACH programme. For example, first, almost one-half (46 per cent) of bursary coaches reported problems in accessing and undertaking requisite coach education courses as a result of difficulties in managing wider employment obligations and resultant time and travel constraints. These problematic time-management issues were exacerbated further for some bursary coaches by the limited frequency of delivery of relevant 'core' and 'youth' coach education courses in specific geographical locales. Similarly, one-quarter (25 per cent) of bursary coaches reported comparable accessibility constraints in relation to the locations and timings of club placement activities. Second, and perhaps more problematically, around 40 per cent of all first-year bursary coaches experienced a lengthy time-lag of more than six months between 'signing-up' for participation in the COACH programme and successfully accessing or being allocated a placement club. This limited availability of club placements was underscored by the lack of initial 'buy-in' to the programme among many Premier League and Football League clubs outside of London and the West Midlands, and had a strong impact on limiting opportunities for bursary coaches to fully engage with the COACH programme and to consequently engender a series of personal and professional benefits of the kind outlined above. Third, and finally, a significant number of bursary coaches and club mentors identified an apparent lack of ongoing communication, guidance and follow-up support for bursary coaches and clubs on the part of COACH programme organisers. This was felt to have led to a lack of organisational clarity with regard to the roles and responsibilities of bursary coaches and placement clubs with regard to: establishing placements, providing mentoring and support, preferred session activities, gaining additional CRB and first-aid certification, offering session payment and expectations towards permanent employment opportunities. Further, a number of bursary coaches reported on the lack of ongoing opportunities to liaise with COACH programme organisers or meet with other bursary coaches to exchange information and reflect on shared experiences. While much of these issues were underscored by some key financial and human resource issues, it nonetheless reflected poorly on the capacity of the programme organisers to realise their inclusionary vision and meant that many bursary coaches and club mentors felt isolated and detached from the national roll-out of the first year programme.

Despite these more critical assertions outlined above, it is also clear that the capacity of the COACH programme to engender key beneficial impacts for bursary coaches has been greatly enhanced where senior coaching staff and club mentors at participating clubs have expressed more 'open' and 'progressive' attitudes and have ensured strong organisational 'buy-in' to the aims and delivery of the programme. Central to this process has been the establishment of a socially supportive and inclusive learning environment for bursary coaches and a strong recognition of and adherence to the value of cultural diversity in the coaching workplace. It is here, at these more 'enlightened' and 'forward thinking' clubs, where there is arguably greater potential to engender both quantitative and qualitative benefits in relation to the recruitment of bursary (and other BME) coaches more broadly. It is arguably the case too that these clubs might also be best positioned to attract and develop talented young players from a broader range of BME and White European backgrounds, and for whom expressions of racial identity and experiences of everyday multiculturalism are the norm. Here, in the competitive market-place of youth academy football, it might just be those clubs who are most reflective of – and understanding of the nuances within – cultural diversity, that are the most likely to win out overall.

Finally, it can be argued that, taken together, the wider literature and specific evaluation findings presented in this chapter have some significant transferability within and across other sporting contexts. In particular, they have generated some clear 'learning points' which might have key implications for NGBs, sports clubs and sports practitioners seeking to address the under-representation of BME coaches in their respective sports. To this end, the development of programmes designed to increase representation and ensure equality of opportunities and outcomes for BME coaches might wish to consider implementing the following theoretically grounded and empirically informed practical recommendations. First, programmes of this kind should seek to ensure that participants are recruited from a broad range of ethnic, educational, employment, playing and coaching backgrounds, and that coach educators adopt a culturally sensitive and inclusive operational approach to the delivery of coach education courses. This will help to address key demographic targets, ensure equitable treatment and broaden the diversity of sports and non-sports skill sets within the coaching workforce. Second, programmes of this kind should conduct a mapping exercise of available coach education courses and ensure that participants are informed, supported and subsidised to attend relevant courses at times and locations which enable attendance. This will help to increase accessibility, quicken the pace of completion of coaching qualifications, and consequently maximise key beneficial impacts for newly qualified coaches. Third, programmes of this kind should make efforts to actively encourage sports clubs and other sports providers in multicultural locales to 'buy-in' to the aims and objectives of establishing a more culturally diverse coaching workforce. This 'buy-in' is likely to be greatly enhanced by the establishment of a clear, co-ordinated and centrally driven process of human and resource support and the production of a standardised guide document for placement clubs and coaches which include a clear checklist of good practice in relation to management, communication and mentoring activities. And, finally, programmes of this kind should embed from the beginning a clear process of external monitoring and evaluation of key inputs, outputs and outcomes of programme involvement. These processes of data collection of analysis will help enable a shift from speculative assertion to empirical evidence and inform programme stakeholders of the success (or otherwise) of 'positive action' efforts to challenge and disrupt those longstanding and deeply embedded processes and practices of institutional discrimination which underpin ongoing racial inequalities in coaching in sport.

Critical questions

1. Does your club, organisation or sport feature a representative number of BME coaches?
2. What are the key barriers faced by BME coaches in your club, organisation or sport, and how do you know this?
3. How might your club, organisation or sport conduct research to evaluate the experiences of BME coaches and identify barriers to their progression?
4. How might your club, organisation or sport implement measures to recruit and support the development of BME coaches?

5. What are the key barriers to implementing measures to recruit and support the development of BME coaches in your club, organisation or sport, and how might you overcome these?
6. How might your club, organisation or sport better utilise the social and technical skill sets of BME coaches to develop young players from a diverse range of backgrounds?

References

Back, L,. Crabbe, T. & Solomos, J. (2001). *The changing face of football: racism, identity and multiculture in the English game*. Oxford: Berg.

Bradbury, S. (2013). Institutional racism, whiteness and the under-representation of minorities in leadership positions in football in Europe. *Soccer and Society*, 14 (3), 296–314.

Bradbury, S. (2014a). *Ethnic minorities and coaching in elite level football in England: a call to action*. Sports People's Think Tank, FARE Network and Loughborough University.

Bradbury, S. (2014b). *An evaluation of the FA COACH bursary programme: activities, experiences, benefits and challenges*. Loughborough University.

Bradbury, S. (2015). *Levels of BME coaches in professional football: 1st annual follow up report (October 2015)*. A report prepared by Loughborough University on behalf of the Sports People's Think Tank.

Bradbury, S., Amara, M., Garcia, B. & Bairner, A. (2011). *Representation and structural discrimination in football in Europe: the case of minorities and women*. Loughborough University and the FARE Network.

Bradbury, S., Van Sterkenburg, J. & Mignon, P. (2014). *Cracking the glass ceiling? Level of representation of 'visible' minorities and women in leadership and coaching in football in Europe and the experiences of elite level 'visible' minority coaches*. Loughborough University and the Football Against Racism in Europe Network.

Burdsey, D. (2007). *British Asians and football: culture, identity and exclusion*. London: Routledge.

13

CANDIDATES' EXPERIENCES OF ELITE FA COACH EDUCATION

Tracking the journey

Robyn L. Jones, Wayne Allison and Jake Bailey

Introduction

In recent years, there has been a significant increase in both the provision of coach education programmes and their evaluation (e.g. Chesterfield *et al.*, 2010; Nelson *et al.*, 2013). While this body of literature has provided scholars and practitioners with valuable knowledge about the role and nature of such programmes, little is known about how coaches experience them. This is not only in terms of their structure, content and assessment (Jones *et al.*, 2004; Taylor & Garratt, 2010), but also in relation to coaches' personal knowledge construction and how that knowledge is transferred into practice. The inadequacy of current coach education programmes to recognise such dynamics, particularly as related to issues of relevancy, was recently reiterated by Piggott (2012), who contended that coaches, across all sporting contexts, continue to place greater value on experiential learning than on formal coach education. Such courses, then, play only a minor role in the wider process of coach development and 'are often treated in a rather instrumental fashion by coaches who rarely learn or implement any new ideas' (Piggott, 2012: 538). Hence, they are continuously considered to be 'fine in theory' but, and crucially, largely divorced from the messy realities of practice (Jones *et al.*, 2012).

Relatedly, there has been a paucity of critical inquiry into the latent and unintended learning that takes place on coach education courses; that is, learning which is not immediately apparent in behaviour but which manifests later when suitable circumstances appear, and learning which has been unplanned and unforeseen. Highlighting such variability of outcome, Roy *et al.* (2010) found that coaches' learning from a single certification module ranged from confusion, to an overload of information, to affirmation of existing practice. Subsequently, although we know that coaches increase their knowledge from formal coach education courses, little information exists on precisely what they learn, in addition to how their ways of knowing develop. This includes issues of how they learn what they learn, to where and why they learn it (if at all). It is a knowledge gap exacerbated by the general absence of temporal research into coach education, and of the importance of considering the various processes that influence it (Cushion *et al.*, 2010). This particularly relates to paying more attention to the practices, people, regimes of competence, communities and boundaries that serve as the creators of who coaches become and who they think they are (Wenger, 2010).

The general purpose of this study was to map the knowledge development of candidates enrolled on an 18-month elite-level FA coach education course. This general aim was addressed through a number of mutually informing objectives. These related to: exploring what the candidates learned from the course and how they learned it; the principal catalysts for change; what the candidates considered to be the strengths and limitations of the course in terms of content, delivery, and assessment; and what role (if any) the tutors played in these developments.

In terms of organisation, following this introduction, the structure of the coach education course undertaken by the candidates is summarised. The methods used within the study are outlined, together with the procedure and the process of data analysis. The results are then cited and subsequently discussed. Finally, a reflective conclusion is presented, inclusive of possible implications for future coach education practice.

The FA case in question: the course structure

The coach education course under study is recognised as the highest qualification obtainable within Association Football. The syllabus was principally constructed by the sport's international federation, although national governing bodies (NGBs) possess a degree of agency in how the recommended components are delivered. The programme was 18 months in duration, with candidates being primarily assessed against a competency framework. An overseas 'group visit' was also built into the course, which involved candidates' observations and deconstruction of top-level coaching practice and sporting performances. Furthermore, each candidate was assigned a mentor (on a ratio of 1:3) whose primary role was to support the candidates through the programme.

The programme itself comprised four key content areas: (1) communication; (2) leadership; (3) management; and (4) business and finance. These were, in turn, divided into seven modules spaced with planned frequency throughout the programme. Each module, excluding the group study, was delivered during three-day 'residential' workshops. The time between the residentials was intended to allow for reflection on received content, and for its practical application in context. The seventh and final module culminated with an expected 'graduation' from the course.

Methods, procedure and data analysis

Methods

The precise methods used within the study included video diaries and focus group interviews. Video diaries are often considered a way for participants to frame and represent their own lives. Their use in this project, then, represented an effort to empower the candidate participants; enabling them to tell their own stories, and represent their own situations in relation to their experiences of the coach education programme undertaken. While recognising that no actual escape from the project's purpose or hierarchy was possible, what was hoped for were less 'mediated' representations of the candidates' selves (Pini, 2001).

Semi-structured group interviews were also conducted with the coaches to explore their personal understandings of their course-related learning and development. Being semi-structured in nature, the interviews allowed responses within a framework of questions while also granting a degree of freedom for the candidates to talk about what was important for them (Morgan, 1988).

Procedure (and participants)

The procedure involved tracking a group of 20 candidates through their elite coach education experience. Each candidate was allocated an iPad for recording individual reflections and encouraged to frequently do so. Additionally, four sets of focus group interviews were carried out with the candidates during their time on the course. The research design was progressive, in that, in addition to the study's stated aims, the periodic focus group interviews were loosely structured on issues raised from candidates' video diaries. In this way, the research was flexible in terms of following certain themes identified as important and meaningful by the candidates. In total, 18 focus group interviews were carried out with the candidate coaches, while 19 video diaries were also received. Once a video diary was received or focus group interview recorded, the data were transcribed verbatim before being subject to a process of analysis (described below).

Data analysis

Inductive procedures were broadly used to examine and categorise the data gathered from both the video diaries and the focus groups. The principal purpose was to identify common themes as related to the aims of the study, while also paying heed to any unexpected features (Charmaz, 2006). Hence, a 'constant comparative method' (Glaser & Strauss, 1967) was employed to ascertain similarities and differences within the data. More specifically, and in line with Charmaz (2006), a process of focused coding was undertaken where earlier identified codes or signifiers were used to further examine the data, thus refining initial assumptions. These were then used to build more generalisable statements that transcended specific instances and times (Charmaz, 2006). This later phase also coincided with greater attempts to analyse what the data actually meant, emphasising the interpretive nature of the research. The constructed categorisations provide the structure for the results section.

Results

Perceived relevance of course content, and the need for security

Although, evidence existed that the candidates valued both the acquisition (i.e. the 'speakers' and 'taught content') as well as the participation (e.g. group discussion) aspects of the course, there was a general feeling that the content to which they were exposed lacked a degree of relevance. Hence, there was a general call for the content to be better 'related to the jobs we are actually doing'. One aspect that made this challenging was that, while the course existed as the pinnacle of coach education within the sport, the candidates nevertheless worked in vastly differing contexts. The following comments were reflective of the common currency in this regard:

> I think a lot of time we speak about the elite stuff ... probably too much and doesn't really cover nuts and bolts ... it only covers the top end.

> It's not relevant to where we're actually working.

Despite the course being framed in terms of the need for candidates to 'read themselves into the content', many found this hard to do. Comments like the following were indicative of such a perception:

> We just sat there, and it was information overkill.

> I've really not gained anything from today.... I don't see the relevance of what we've done today.

> The links can be quite tough to make ... it's hard to make those links sometimes.

> They're asking us to do stuff we're not going to use.

Not all the content-related elements, however, were considered as lacking relevance. Many of the coaches confirmed that they were able to 'take things from various sessions'. Such learning, however, appeared largely restricted to relatively minor practicalities as opposed to developing a new 'way of thinking' ('little bits that have been said, I can take back and it's broadened my horizons'; 'the course does give you little things, no doubt'; 'you take bits from everything'). Consequently, although the candidates were aware of the need to make sense of the information given within their own contexts, there remained a pre-occupation among them for very practical 'know-how' material which they could, more or less, immediately apply. This included an explicit desire for more speakers 'who have done our job' and 'who know what it's like, and done it', as opposed to people from other walks of life. The knowledge desired, therefore, was very viable, to a degree safe, and convenient, as opposed to being abstract or conceptually troublesome. In addition to information which they could easily relate to, this tendency towards the functional reflected a wish for a general re-affirmation or incremental development of existing beliefs among the candidates, as opposed to any conceptual shift in thinking ('not a change in my behaviour ... just a bit of confidence in what [I] actually do'). Hence, they appeared to actively resist information which opened out additional fields and frames of reference, preferring instead the less risky option of better developing what they already knew.

Supporting this thesis of the requirement for security (of operating within existing frames of reference), what the candidates valued most about the programme was the collective social experience ('a big part of it for me is getting away'). Of considerable ongoing importance here was the reassurance function of the course. In the words of some of the coaches:

> You come here and you speak, and everybody's in the same boat ... it reassures you that you're not the only one.

> You find a little bit of solace here.

> It made me realise that the problems I've got, everybody else has got ... I'm not on my own.

This perception of the course as a haven or refuge of sorts assumed even greater magnitude as the programme progressed. This was because, as the insecure nature of their work became ever more apparent, by the end of the course many of the coaches had either lost or feared for their jobs ('you know each other now; and you're under stress, so it [the 'bond' between them] is stronger now'). This was often couched in the desire to learn from each other, to discover each other's experiences ('you can learn an awful lot from the people who are here'; 'I've learned far more from people's actual experiences'). Hence, echoing the above point regarding the coaches' wish for more relevant content (i.e. 'practical' or even 'anecdotal'), the candidates valued hearing others' stories that affirmed their own insecure and stressful experiences. In the words of two candidates:

> It's an affirmation that what you're doin' is the right thing, so it's not just a sharing of ideas.

> I feel better coming here today, coz people have the same problems you have.

The competency assessment structure and a desire for peer learning

The course was based around the coaches realising a set of given competencies – a format which the candidates found problematic. Such difficulties were multifaceted and comprised: (1) the competencies being sometimes difficult to comprehend; (2) the coaches not fully understanding how the competencies should be evidenced; (3) a perception of duplication between many of the competencies; in addition to (4) doubting their relevance for everyday coaching. The final issue was considered the most problematic due to the competencies' often decontextualised nature. Consequently, the candidates held an instrumental view of the competencies, engaging with them largely superficially, limiting their impact on candidates' working practices.

The coaches believed that an alternative structure for learning would have been of greater benefit for them; one more grounded in collaborative small-group work. This is not to say that the candidates didn't value the new information given in the speaker-led sessions, just that they would have preferred more time spent in group work to better discuss how to make such content personally applicable ('I don't think we actually unpick things enough'; 'we're not following it through'; 'we've just ticked a box and haven't followed it through'). Allied to this was the candidates' desire to be allowed to learn more from each other, thus formalising some of the valued informal learning evident ('you can learn an awful lot from the people who are here'). Indeed, there was considerable evidence of peer learning taking place in the 'social' opportunities available, outside of the formal learning context – something again that emphasised their desire to hear each other's solutions.

Candidate views of course mentors and mentoring

The candidates were equivocal when talking about their course mentors and the latter's role in their learning. Despite being in regular (usually text) contact, some of the coaches, due to their hectic schedules, found it hard to make time to be with their mentors ('I find that I've got so much to do, it's hard to keep real contact'). There was also a perception that the mentors should be located physically closer to them ('Geographically, it really should be better … they haven't done that very well'; 'it's great when he gets here, when he gets here…'). On the other hand, there was a perception by some that their mentors were not visible or active enough in setting up meeting times (the onus to do this was largely placed on the mentors). In this respect, the candidates appeared to accept little responsibility for the mentorship process, it being viewed as something they were subject to rather than actively engaged with. Similarly, there was also a desire for more direction and leadership from the mentors, which led some to question whether the mentors were really clear in their roles. In the words of the coaches:

If he doesn't know what we're meant to be doing, what chance have I got?

I'm not sure whether the mentors are actually sure themselves ... they were [just] as confused.

There was also unease that the candidates had not received a consistent level of mentoring; some had many visits and good support, others less so ('there's got to be one message'; 'there's been some crossed wires, for sure'). This situation was not helped by some candidates losing and gaining mentors mid-course.

Another area of concern for the candidates was the mentors' knowledge base in actually being able to help them with their practice ('have any of the tutors been a manager?'; 'A lot of them don't work in [our] environment ... the tutors are too far removed from that specific area'). This was not to question the mentors' sincerity, commitment or abilities, but just whether they were adequately grounded in an understanding of the candidates' roles and realities. Consequently, the candidates viewed the mentors instrumentally ('I just need to know what to do to pass this course'), with the mentors' premier (in some cases only) role being to assist in the gathering and explaining of the competencies. There was also a belief that the mentors needed to be chosen a little more carefully in relation to candidates' individual needs ('if the course is bespoke, then maybe the mentors can be too') – something that became increasingly clear as the course progressed, with some relationships flourishing while others proved problematic.

Implications for coach education: discussion and conclusion

Echoing the findings of previous work (e.g. Cushion *et al.*, 2010), the results from this study highlighted the importance and considerable influence of informal experience upon coach learning. Indeed, the candidates wanted more official opportunities for discussion-type activities to further develop their learning. Allied to, or a part of, this desire was a wish to hear from other practitioners or coaches (in addition to each other) who had 'been there and done it', a request couched under the stated desire for more 'relevant' content. Although the question of relevancy (or the perception of relevancy) has previously been cited and discussed as crucial for candidates' engagement on coach education courses (e.g. Jones *et al.*, 2012; Nelson *et al.*, 2013), the call here appeared more complex than on initial reflection. On one level, it could be viewed as a rather straightforward request for applicability of subject content, for 'tools' and 'tips' (or 'war stories') immediately useable in practice. From such an interpretation, the course could be judged to have failed to move or alter the coaches' fundamental ideas and frames of reference about coaching and how to go about it. What they wanted were just other (perhaps better) ways and means to do what they already did. The work here supports the conclusions of Cushion *et al.* (2010: i), who stated that 'most learning is undertaken within a cluster of ideas or experiences, or the result of a "default" view' of coaching. As other research has also postulated (e.g. Christensen, 2013), influencing such biographically developed views-of-the-world among coaches is a complex, time-consuming task. Perhaps one that requires considerably more than a single or even a set of isolated professional preparation programmes.

From another perspective, however, this desire for 'relevancy' (and the importance attached to the interactions incidental to the course) could somewhat be explained by a need for security. That elite coaching is an insecure profession is not in doubt, which makes the issue's conceptual and empirical neglect by researchers all the more surprising. Although Olusoga and colleagues (2012) examined some of the 'stressors' experienced by elite coaches, their psychological theorising and recommended coping mechanisms presented a very functional, emotionally devoid account of heartfelt experiences. In a recent symposium, however, building on the work of Jones and Wallace (2005, 2006), the issue of coaches' ambiguous work was recently taken up by Ronglan (2013), Mesquita (2013) and Jones (2013) from a social and relational perspective. Here, coaching was directly theorised in terms of its insecure nature; an insecurity which ranged from the opaqueness of athlete learning, through the vagaries of temporality, to the unpredictability and relative unmanageability of game-related contexts. Such ambiguity and pathos create great insecurity and instability for coaches, inevitably generating a working context characterised by constant negotiation, struggle, micro-politics and 'plays of power' (Jones & Wallace, 2006). The candidates' desire for a perceived relevancy of content, then, could be perceived as a need to hear like-minded messages they could immediately relate to. In this respect, the course was considered a kind of sanctuary for the candidates; a safe, supportive place where they could sometimes retreat, away from the everyday pressures of the job; a place where they could feel they were not unique and distinct in facing the stressful problems of practice which often stretched far beyond sport performance issues. Indeed, in many ways, we consider this the most interesting finding of the work, in that the course seemed to provide a latent function in providing a 'community of security' for the coaches, something they valued over and above every other aspect of their educational experience.

A second finding of note was dissatisfaction among the candidate coaches regarding the competency framework used as the principal means of course assessment. The perceived decontextualisation of practice resulted in the evidencing of such competencies taking on purely instrumental characteristics; that is, they were merely engaged with by the coaches to 'pass the test'. The generalisation of practice engendered through the approach appeared to provide the coaches' criticisms of the course as lacking a degree of relevance greater credence. Even though the candidates could be perceived as doing similar jobs, the differences in individual workplaces, which, in turn, impacted on precise roles, precluded any 'general fit'.

In many ways, then, the notion of given competencies holding good across coaching organisations and clubs of different size, operating at different levels with different histories and objectives, tended to contradict the candidates' personal experiences. The discontent regarding the framework also stretched to confusion surrounding issues of 'competence identification' and related assessment.

A final principal finding relates to the candidates' perceptions of the course mentors, a supportive facility or role which has been heavily advocated for coach learning (Cushion *et al.*, 2010: Nelson *et al.*, 2013). In terms of structure, although each candidate had access to a particular mentor, the learning relationships established were not altogether unproblematic. For example, despite a general perception of improvement and knowledge development, the coaches' experiences as mentees were varied. The primary problem related to a perception of the mentors, and hence of themselves as mentees, as being unsure of their particular roles. This is an issue prevalent in many elite coach education programmes; that is, an under-theorisation and general lack of understanding of the mentoring relationship. Consequently, although the idea and language of mentorship has increasingly become prevalent in the coaching literature (e.g. Nelson *et al.*, 2013), with some exceptions, the concept appears to have remained at the assumed or even abstract level of rhetoric. Clearly, then, this is an aspect which needs considerable attention.

The purpose of this chapter was to explore and highlight the experiences of coaches on an 18-month elite coach education programme. The results both support and build upon existing work. In relation to the latter (with which we are naturally more concerned), the most relevant finding concerns the value of the programme as a 'community of security' for practitioners who operate in a very insecure world. The obvious subsequent implication for coach education lies in the need to both recognise this insecurity and to better engage with it. This, of course, is not a straightforward demand for such courses to include 'anti-stress' or 'stress-coping' sessions or the like, even though there may be an argument for greater coach care to take place. Rather, it is a call for such professional preparation programmes to help coaches better accept and live with the complexity of their positions, through giving them realistic ways of dealing with it. This was the purpose behind Jones and colleagues' (Jones & Wallace, 2005, 2006; Jones *et al.*, 2013) reconceptualisation of coaching as orchestration; an effort to provide more practical guidance for coaches to make the most of what they are able to do (and how they can do it), without expecting to achieve unrealistic directive control as they navigate the turbulent waters of their working lives. Doing so harbours better potential to understand and engage with the some of the more gritty realities of coaching, which coach education programmes have thus far failed to adequately address.

Critical questions

1. Consider the value of competency framework-oriented courses in your own learning. What are/were their strengths and weaknesses?
2. How realistic is the notion of a 'community of security' for elite-level coaches? Should coach education courses take account of such factors or be more concerned with content knowledge?

3.   If coaching contexts are so unique and diverse, what is the value of a universal mentoring programme for elite coaches?
4.   Consider the relative merits of 'acquisition' and 'participation' forms of developing knowledge.

Note

An earlier developed version of this chapter was published as a paper in the *European Journal of Human Movement* (June, 2014).

References

Charmaz, K. (2006). *Constructing grounded theory: a practical guide through qualitative analysis.* Thousand Oaks, CA: Sage.

Chesterfield, G., Potrac, P. & Jones, R.L. (2010). 'Studentship' and 'impression management': coaches' experiences of an advanced soccer coach education award. *Sport, Education and Society*, 15 (3), 299–314.

Christensen, M.K. (2013). Outlining a typology of sports coaching careers: paradigmatic trajectories and ideal career types among high performance sports coaches. *Sports Coaching Review*, 2 (2), 98–113.

Cushion, C., Nelson, L., Armour, K., Lyle, J., Jones, R., Sandford, R. & O'Callaghan, C. (2010). *Coach learning and development: a review of literature.* Leeds: Sports Coach UK.

Glaser, B.G. & Strauss, A.L. (1967). *The discovery of grounded theory: strategies for qualitative research.* Chicago, IL: Aldine.

Jones, R.L. (2013). Towards a theory of coaching: the learning order. Invited presentation given at the European College of Sport Science (ECSS), Barcelona, Spain, 26–29 June.

Jones, R.L. & Wallace, M. (2005). Another bad day at the training ground: coping with ambiguity in the coaching context. *Sport, Education and Society*, 10 (1), 119–134.

Jones. R.L. & Wallace, M. (2006). The coach as orchestrator. In R.L. Jones (ed.), *The sports coach as educator: re-conceptualising sports coaching* (pp. 51–64). London: Routledge.

Jones, R.L., Armour, K.M. & Potrac, P. (2004). *Sports coaching cultures: from practice to theory.* London: Routledge.

Jones, R.L., Morgan, K. & Harris, K. (2012). Developing coaching pedagogy: seeking a better integration of theory and practice. *Sport, Education and Society*, 17 (3), 313–329.

Jones, R.L., Bailey, J. & Thompson, I. (2013). Ambiguity, noticing, and orchestration: further thoughts on managing the complex coaching context. In P. Potrac, W. Gilbert & J. Denison (eds), *The Routledge handbook of sports coaching* (pp. 271–283). London: Routledge.

Mesquita, I. (2013). Towards a theory of coaching: the temporal order. Invited presentation given at the European College of Sport Science (ECSS), Barcelona, Spain, 26–29 June.

Morgan, D.L. (1988). *Focus groups as qualitative research.* Newbury Park, CA: Sage.

Nelson, L., Cushion, C. & Potrac, P. (2013). Enhancing the provision of coach education: the recommendation of UK coaching practitioners. *Physical Education and Sport Pedagogy*, 18 (2), 204–218.

Olusoga, P., Maynard, I., Hays, K. & Butt, J. (2012). Coaching under pressure: a study of Olympic coaches. *Journal of Sport Sciences*, 30 (3), 229–239.

Piggott, D. (2012). Coaches' experiences of formal coach education: a critical sociological investigation. *Sport, Education and Society*, 17 (4), 535–554.

Pini, M. (2001). *Video diaries: questions of authenticity and fabrication*. Available: www.latrobe. edu.au/screeningthepast/firstrelease/fr1201/mpfr13a.htm, accessed 13 December 2014.

Ronglan, L.T. (2013). Towards a theory of coaching: the insecurity order. Invited presentation given at the European College of Sport Science (ECSS), Barcelona, Spain, 26–29 June.

Roy, M., Beaudoin, S. & Spallanzani, C. (2010). *Analyse des connaissances des entraîneurs inscrits à une formation « Introduction à la compétition – Partie B » en matière de planification d'entraînement*. Sherbrooke, Québec: Université de Sherbrooke, Faculté d'éducation physique et sportive.

Taylor, B. & Garratt, D. (2010). The professionalisation of sports coaching: relations of power, resistance and compliance. *Sport, Education and Society*, 15 (1), 121–139.

Wenger, E. (2010). Knowledgeability in landscapes of practice: from curriculum to identity. Presentation given at the Society for Research into Higher Education Annual Research Conference, 14–16 December.

PART IV
Summary

14

FUTURE DIRECTIONS IN COACHING RESEARCH

Andy Cale and Andrew Abraham

Introduction

A key purpose of this book was to highlight and consider selected contemporary issues related to sports coaching in the modern world. Furthermore, the intention was also to raise awareness and provoke thought and discussion around potential future research questions in and around this simple, yet complex, concept of coaching.

This book has examined a wide range of different coach education and development themes and has described the different journeys from research question to practical application. The purpose of this final section of the book is to briefly summarise the major issues raised in each of the preceding chapters and then to consider the key issues and questions facing both governing bodies and those conducting research in the coaching domain.

Consequently, it is hoped that professional practitioners, whether they be researchers, coaches or system developers, will be provoked and encouraged to examine their specific role in helping the profession develop.

Chapter 1: The Football Association's coach education and development programme: research informing practice – Wayne Allison

This chapter not only set the context for coaching research within a specific governing body, The Football Association (The FA), but also identified and presented a model for the research process which provides the information for evidence-based decision-making.

Initially, this work described the detail contained within The FA Coaching Strategy 2013–17. This strategy, like many others, was logically constructed and based on the original work from the UK Coaching Framework. This framework generated five key pillars and 15 specific areas of focus and provides a logical integration for coaching research with the other components of a world-leading coaching system.

The chapter continues to outline and describe the coaching research strategy cycle used by The FA. With the generation of robust data and effective communication across and within any organisation, research can provide the basis and act as a vehicle for non-biased and meaningful feedback on all aspects of the coaching system. The role and function of a coaching research manager is explored in detail.

Current issue

By considering the many different aspects of the coaching framework, has the 'big picture' of what coaching 'actually is' been lost? Has focus moved more to the underpinning structures and processes rather than the actual 'art or science' of the coaching act?

Consideration for a governing body

Which aspects of our current coaching system require immediate and priority attention? What evidence do we actually have to help with our decision-making?

Consideration for research

Should more research be conducted around the 'inputs' to the coaching process or the 'outputs' related the players and teams involved?

Chapter 2: Benchmarking sport coach education and development: using programme theories to examine and evolve current practice – Julian North

This chapter describes an interesting perspective on benchmarking sport coach education and development that was based on the early work of Duffy and colleagues. Benchmarking compares principles, processes and practices to industry bests or best practices from other leading experts and organisations.

The FA case study reported explained how the researchers adopted a 'critical realist' approach to underpin the benchmarking process. This was innovative and challenging and linked the concepts of programme theory, contexts (C), mechanisms (M) and outcomes (O). For coach education, the realist evaluators talked about 'CMO configurations' being the basis for programme theory development and evaluation. The results of the research were fascinating and provided a detailed insight as to the limitations and value of simple benchmarking activities.

The benchmarking process illustrated does not seek to provide a current state of the nation view on English football and how it compares to other major European football nations and major sports. What it does, instead, is to provide a new way of thinking about coaching as 'programme theories' and how they are 'layered' in different components parts.

Current issue

Simple benchmarking activities may not accurately describe complex coaching structures and outcomes.

Consideration for a governing body

How may governing bodies adopt meaningful benchmarking activities? Considering 'World Best' is always useful. What principles can be adopted? Will copying systems work in different sports and countries?

Consideration for research

How can researchers best capture and compare complex coaching systems?

Chapter 3: CPD provision for the football coaching workforce: what can we learn from other professional fields and what are the implications? – Kathleen Armour, Mark Griffiths and Alexander De Lyon

This chapter delivered a brief summary of some of the continuous professional development (CPD) literature that currently exists in the professions of physiotherapy and teaching and questioned how this may relate to the profession of sports (football) coaching.

Historically, there was some evidence within football that CPD courses lack relevance in both content and design. Despite the differences between the professions, overall there were similarities in relation to CPD, including the prevalence of informal learning, lack of time and management support for professional learning, and an inadequate CPD evaluation process that tends to evaluate attendance rather than learning.

The authors concluded that football coaching can learn from the errors made in other professional fields and by developing a new model, add something novel to the wider CPD research evidence base. In addition, the value of needs-led CPD was highlighted along with the importance of matching CPD learning to the developmental stage of each coach.

Current issue

The concept of CPD is often considered as an addition to the mainstream of courses and qualifications and often sits apart from the original design of professional learning systems.

Consideration for a governing body

How do governing bodies ensure that their CPD programmes are well planned, coherent, challenging, relevant and progressive? Do the system developers fully understand and appreciate the needs of their individual learners?

Consideration for research

How robust are the evaluation mechanisms in place to monitor the effectiveness of specific CPD packages? To what degree do the various CPD programmes balance the need for formal, informal and non-formal learning?

Chapter 4: Quality assurance procedures in coach education – William Taylor and Ryan Groom

Sport organisations in the UK must commit to treat their coaches and other members of the coaching community as 'customers in their own right', and consider the quality of the services they consume. This chapter considers the procedures and practices employed by governing bodies of sport in their efforts to quality assure (QA) their coach education schemes and delivery. Their review of literature draws from schemes and processes outside of sport.

The use of visiting inspectors and assessors working within a number of differing QA frameworks is now commonplace and it is apparent that there has been a change in emphasis, moving from a notion of 'quality assurance' towards one of 'quality enhancement'. The significant change is that the role of the inspector is now evolving towards one of knowledge exchange and the sharing of good practices and away from inspection against a set of pre-designated criteria.

Any move away from a sterile representation of QA towards one that sees it as an opportunity to enhance the value of coach tutors will require both a cultural shift and an investment in those taking on new responsibilities.

Current issue

Quality assurance and quality enhancement can be positive and developmental processes for coach education schemes.

Consideration for a governing body

Do governing bodies have the right people with the right skill sets to perform these roles effectively? Is the 'investment' and 'culture' supportive of enhancement processes?

Consideration for research

How will researchers measure and evaluate the impact of improved QA procedures?

Chapter 5: Task analysis of coach developers: applications to The FA Youth Coach Educator role – Andrew Abraham

Very little is known about the role definition and practice of coach educators or developers (assuming these people are different, when often they are not). Consequently, very little is also known about the knowledge and skills required to complete the role.

This chapter focused on gaining an understanding of what the required knowledge and skills were through interviews with and observation of practising coach educators. These knowledge and skills reflect both the more thoughtful and the more intuitive demands of the role of a coach educator across six task domains: understand the context; understand the coach; understand adult learning; understand coaching curriculum; understand process and practice; and understand self.

In completing this project the chapter offers definition of skills and knowledge across these six tasks. Given that these results were obtained from high-level coach educators they essentially benchmark the role, providing a basis from which self-analysis and professional development decisions can be made.

Some insight is offered as to how this work led to the development of a bespoke Postgraduate Certificate in Coach Education for The FA. This has offered formal professional development for a group of FA Youth Coach Educators.

Current issue

Relatively little is known about skills and knowledge required to be a coach educator. Accordingly, relatively little is known about what the formal and non-formal CPD needs are for coach educators.

Consideration for a governing body

Do governing bodies have a clear view on what type of coach educator they require, what goals the coach educators are working towards and/or what type of professional development they need to offer to their coach educators?

Consideration for research

How will research be able to continue to unpack and understand the role of coach educators? More detail relating to the demands of each task domain and the required knowledge and skills of coach educators is also needed to more accurately inform professional development methods.

Chapter 6: The application of reflective practice: reflective learning in the education and practices of FA football coaches – Jenny Moon

This chapter introduced the concept of reflective practice and considered its application to the game of Association Football. More specifically, the process was described, considered and utilised as a learning mechanism to help the development of coach educators, coaches and players.

'Reflection' as a term is constructed to describe a general pattern of cognitive behaviour that is seen as helpful to learning and professional practice. It was explained that there are difficulties in researching a constructed term such as 'reflection' or 'reflective learning' since different people interpret the term in different ways.

The FA case study required the author to devise and deliver a 'reflective practice' workshop to coach educators where the learning outcomes were: to demonstrate articulate reflective thinking at a reasonable depth; to consider the potential value of a more reflective approach in professional practice for coaches and players; to specify some practical ways in which they can introduce reflective learning into everyday work.

Current issue

Reflective practice is a skill that requires time, commitment and repetition in order to achieve optimal results.

Consideration for a governing body

At what point in the coach education programme should coaches be introduced to this skill? How may 'reflection' help coach educators in their own professional development?

Consideration for research

Reflection requires the coach to 'notice' and analyse key events. How can coaches be helped to 'notice' important episodes within training and match environments?

Chapter 7: Delivering The FA Grassroots Club Mentor Programme: mentors' experiences of practice – Paul Potrac

In the domain of sports coaching, we continue to know relatively little about how mentors might develop an appropriate mix of social, cultural and symbolic capital that allows them to obtain the 'buy-in', trust and respect of the mentee. Given this state of affairs, there has been an increasing recognition of the need to move beyond superficial and one-dimensional accounts of this activity by better investigating the everyday realities of mentoring, especially in terms of the concerns, questions, reactions and coping strategies of all involved.

The purpose of this study was to investigate the mentors' subjective experiences of delivering The FA Grassroots Club Mentor Programme. The results showed that while the mentors' engagements and relationships with others in the club setting were frequently positive and constructive affairs, they were not always entirely unproblematic. Given these initial findings, it was suggested that NGBs may wish to consider how they best facilitate coach educators' and mentors' engagement with individuals and clubs.

Current issue

Mentoring in sports coaching cannot ignore the 'micro-politics' which surrounds and influences any given environment.

Consideration for a governing body

How can sports create the correct culture and climate for mentoring to be successful as an integrated part of its coach education and development programmes?

Consideration for research

How may researchers generate empirical evidence related to the nature of the mentoring process, especially in terms of how it is experienced and understood by all those involved?

Chapter 8: What do coaches learn and can new knowledge be effectively applied? – Eleanor Quested, Paul Appleton and Joan Duda

Quested and colleagues introduced a thought-provoking chapter that linked psychological theories underpinning player motivation to the creation of positive climates and environments. It was explained how coaches have the 'potential' to optimise players' motivation via the coaching climate they create but that in order to do this effectively they must fully understand the concepts and theories underpinning the coaching environment.

The review of literature showed that more 'empowering' coaches tend to coach, communicate and relate to players in a way that is more likely to lead them to feel a sense of autonomy, competence and connectedness.

The case study introduced within the chapter investigated whether coaches could be better prepared and educated in terms of these key motivational states by attending a specific workshop and whether they could then apply the principles underpinning empowerment to their own coaching.

Interestingly, results suggested that the initial understanding of coaches in relation to 'climate' and 'environments' was superficial and, at times, not always aligned with contemporary and scientifically grounded perspectives on the topic areas. However, with an additional workshop, coaches and coach educators developed a better knowledge base which impacted on their coaching behaviour.

Current issue

Can coaches and coach educators be better equipped for their roles if they increase their knowledge base around key psychological constructs?

Consideration for a governing body

Will the production of more knowledgeable coaches lead to the delivery of more 'empowered' players who will be more creative and better decision-makers?

Consideration for research

Do current coach education courses deliver sufficient detail and knowledge to change coach behaviour? How can researchers best detect changes in knowledge and behaviour?

Chapter 9: Examining the impact of The FA Youth Coach Education Programme: evidence of change? – Kathleen Armour, Mark Griffiths and Alexander De Lyon

This chapter reported on a unique and innovative coach education programme (FAYCE) that had attempted to support coaches as learners *in situ*. The rationale of the work was to deliver a personalised and needs-led development programme at the site of coaches' practice.

In terms of coach learning within the club setting, they found that the programme offered a personalised learning experience, and is a good example of a needs-led approach to coach learning. The programme was highly valued for delivering coach education in-house and had facilitated a shift in the way youth coaching is conceived and delivered. Coach learning occurred in three areas: thinking, practice and self-confidence.

In terms of the promotion of effective practice, they found that positive change was a consequence of sustained contact between the FAYCE and club coaches. The FAYCE programme had promoted improved communications between youth football academies and The FA, and indeed coach educators in the programme are increasingly taking up informal mentoring roles within clubs.

Current issue

Effective CPD programmes need time, energy and appropriate resources in order to meet the requirements of the modern learner.

Consideration for a governing body

If these programmes are as successful as they appear, how do governing bodies train and support an expanded coach educator workforce? Is there enough of the right talent that can be developed?

Consideration for research

When considering 'needs-led' programmes, is it the individual 'coach need' or the 'organisational (club) need' that takes priority? How do you best identify these needs?

Chapter 10: Practice activities during coaching sessions in elite youth football and their effect on skill acquisition – Paul R. Ford and Jordan Whelan

This chapter reviews previous research and theory on the practice activities that youth football players engage in during coaching sessions. Following this review, two new research studies are presented that examined practice activities in elite youth football coaching sessions, as well as skill and knowledge acquisition in both coaches and players.

Researchers have made the distinction between and have investigated the proportion of youth coaching session time spent in 'drill' versus 'games-based' activities. One overall aim of The Football Association's range of coaching courses is 'to produce technically excellent and innovative players with exceptional decision-making skills'.

The first new study was designed to investigate whether the amount of games-based activity had increased in 2013 following the implementation by The FA of new coach education courses when compared to the data that was collected in 2007. The second new study examined the effectiveness of a coaching course (Advanced Youth Award or AYA) in changing coach behaviour and, subsequently, player skill acquisition.

Current issue

Coaching courses often have very specific intended outcomes that are not always achieved. The design, delivery and assessment are not always aligned.

Consideration for a governing body

How do governing bodies check that they have achieved their learning outcomes for any given coach education course?

Consideration for research

How do system designers check for the source of behavioural change and advances in professional knowledge?

Chapter 11: Coaching disabled footballers: a study of the coach journey – Annette Stride, Hayley Fitzgerald and Ellie May

Through its coach education programme, The FA signposts a commitment to its broader goal of 'football for everyone' and acknowledges a responsibility to work towards inclusion and anti-discrimination. Indeed, The FA, along with other NGBs, has engaged in focused activities to raise levels of participation and increase performance in sport among disabled people. These activities include supporting coach development, and this chapter specifically considers the nature and structure of The FA's Coaching Disabled Footballers (CDF) course.

The literature review demonstrated that there was a need for focused research exploring the participation, experiences and attitudes of disabled athletes (including footballers) and coaches. The authors then described research that explored the experiences of those involved in organising, delivering and participating in The FA's CDF course.

The findings from this research suggest the CDF course has a number of key strengths and areas for potential development. For example, course participants highlighted how they valued the tutors' knowledge and approach, the combination of practical and theory, the course being relevant, cost and the opportunity to share experiences and concerns with other coaches. Contrastingly, there was some dissatisfaction which highlighted the lack of post-course support, course length and course content.

Current issue

Coaches need to have a greater awareness and understanding of disability-specific issues in relation to their own sport

Consideration for a governing body

Should all governing bodies have their own specific modules and courses which address disability sport or should there be a generic, common approach across sports?

Consideration for research

What is the ideal theory–practice balance in terms of the curriculum content and assessment of disability sport coaching courses?

Chapter 12: The progression of Black and minority ethnic (BME) footballers into coaching in professional football: a case study analysis of the COACH bursary programme – Steven Bradbury

This chapter investigated the COACH bursary programme that was described as a positive action initiative designed to offer support to a number of BME coaches. The aim for the coaches was to achieve high-level coaching qualifications and undertake placement opportunities at professional clubs.

A review of key literature showed that the extent to which the 'super-diversity' of English society is fully represented within the various tiers of professional football remains partial and mixed. A wide range of background contextual, social and constraining factors for the BME coaches were highlighted. These included limited access to and negative experiences of coach education environments, limited opportunities for mentoring and financial support, limited aspirations and engagement, 'racially closed' methods of coach recruitment along with dominant 'insider' networks, conscious and unconscious racial bias and stereotyping and a lack of BME role models.

The information collected helped to 'explore the journeys' of selected coaches through their early coach education experiences as well as to analyse the specific club placements with mentoring and support.

Current issue

Are the structural and cultural processes that combine to form institutional discrimination in coaching fully understood across different sports?

Consideration for a governing body

How best may the management and delivery of 'support programmes' be improved to help achieve the aims and outcomes of specific interventions?

Consideration for research

Is there a detailed understanding of the 'real' and 'perceived' barriers facing BME coaches? What intervention models are most effective within British sport structures?

Chapter 13: Candidates' experiences of elite FA coach education: tracking the journey – Robyn L. Jones, Wayne Allison and Jake Bailey

There has been much criticism of formal coach education courses, and questions have arisen as to the quality of the learning environments and, indeed, the actual amount of learning that has taken place at the individual coach level. Jones and his colleagues argue that although it is known that coaches are able to increase their knowledge from formal coach education courses, more investigation is required about the detail of how they learn, what they learn and where and why they learn it.

The research described in this chapter focused on the 'journey' taken by a number of coaches enrolled on an elite, 18-month coach education course. The results highlighted the importance and considerable influence of informal experience upon coach learning and the coaches' requests for more structured discussion-type activities to support their learning.

The authors conclude by arguing that professional preparation programmes should help coaches better accept and live with the complexity of their positions, through giving them realistic ways of dealing with it.

Current issue

Elite coaches learn in different ways and require individualised and supported programmes.

Consideration for a governing body

At elite levels of coach education, what are the different methods of designing and delivering advanced-level courses? Are course outcomes constructively aligned with content and assessment methods?

Consideration for research

How can research best describe and explain the individual learning journeys at this level? Are elite coaches really different from other elite professionals?

Future directions in coaching research

This book has enabled and provoked the consideration of many different aspects relating to the current research in coach education and development. Indeed, the book was structured with three separate but linked areas: contextual issues; development and support; and impact and practice. What does the future hold for research in these three areas going forward?

Contextual issues

The 'complex and messy' descriptions of sports coaching are accurate and unavoidable due to the wide range of experiences of people and the different domains related to this subject discipline.

Future research must be more specific and precise so that coaching is better understood in all of its different guises. The role and function of a 'full-time professional' must be different to that of a 'part-time volunteer' and therefore closer attention to the 'needs' of the different types of coach in different settings is required as we move to better support 'coaching as a profession'.

Development and support

The concept of 'coach development' has attracted much attention, especially from the professionals involved with adult learning. The requirement to better understand 'individual needs' and how best these can be met is crucial. The integration of formal and informal learning needs further investigation, along with the link to competency development and ownership of the development journey. Governing bodies can establish frameworks and structures, but it is the individual coach that must select the appropriate vehicles for their own learning. The advances in information technology and the various interfaces for coaches and players to enhance their own learning have exciting potential. The balance around how to best utilise the new media while retaining the essence of coaching and human relationships will be an interesting and crucial development.

Impact and practice

The concept of 'coaching effectiveness' without doubt remains a topical and crucial area as we move forward. The criteria for coaching effectiveness are not well defined nor are they easy to determine. Simple indices are often reported without acknowledging the full complexity of the 'coaching process'. Exactly 'how' coaches achieve their specific outcomes and agreed objectives must be better understood and shared for the profession to grow and develop maturity and acceptance.

A desire to improve: governing body, coach and researcher commitment

It is the responsibility of a governing body and all its available infrastructure to support any given game or sport to grow and develop. In the context of sports coaching, governing bodies must ensure that all systems and people are effectively aligned and supported so that they can in turn effectively develop the performers and players under their care.

The individual coach must demonstrate and strive for better professional practice. It is the responsibility of the coach to continue learning every day about the sport and the athlete under consideration. The best coaches are driven by self-improvement and the provision of excellent learning and performance environments for their athletes.

The researcher has obligations to deliver accurate and robust evidence in relation to all aspects of the coaching frameworks and processes involved in this exciting and evolving profession. Furthermore, the researcher also has a responsibility to question and challenge the approaches and processes involved.

INDEX